Sister T

Hope this will be a blessing for your ministry for our children and our people!

Rev. W. J. Webb
April 18, 2017
404-696-8427

The Way out of Darkness

Vital Public Theology

Willie James Webb

AuthorHouse™
1663 Liberty Drive, Suite 200
Bloomington, IN 47403
www.authorhouse.com
Phone: 1-800-839-8640

© 2008 Willie James Webb. All rights reserved.

No part of this book may be reproduced, stored in a retrieval system, or transmitted by any means without the written permission of the author.

First published by AuthorHouse 2/18/2008

ISBN: 978-1-4343-6137-0 (hc)
ISBN: 978-1-4343-3632-3 (sc)

Library of Congress Control Number: 2007906563

Printed in the United States of America
Bloomington, Indiana

This book is printed on acid-free paper.

Contents

Chapter 1
Introduction … 1

Chapter 2
The Vision for Public Theology … 17

Chapter 3
The Theological Perspective … 21

Chapter 4
What Is Public Theology? … 25

Chapter 5
The Problem for Public Theology … 39

Chapter 6
Critical Questions for the Public Theologian … 45

Chapter 7
The Invitation of Public Theology … 49

Chapter 8
Guiding Themes for Public Theology … 53

Chapter 9
Foundations for Biblical Understanding … 59

Chapter 10
The Christian Role in Diversity … 69

Chapter 11
Guides for Ethical Decisions … 91

Guides for Ethical Decisions
Criteria for Ethical Decision-making … 105

Chapter 12
The Therapy of Worship … 109

Chapter 13
The Practice of Public Theology … 117

THE PRACTICE OF PUBLIC THEOLOGY
Human Protective Standards   129

POSITIONS, ADVOCACY, POLICIES AND ACTIONS
For The Establishment of Human Protective Standards   133

CHAPTER 14
Theological Responsibility for Public Policy   149

Chapter 1

Introduction

This book is not intended to be an academically scholarly research written book for hermeneutical debate and discussion. You will not find the usual voluminous superfluous research references and footnotes. The well-written researched enumerated books are often useful for information and scholarly purposes. We are fortunate to have a vast resource of such books available and in our libraries.

This volume, <u>The Way Out of Darkness – Through Public Theology</u>, is intended to be written in a language and style that can be easily understood by the laity and persons who are not necessarily seminary trained. This book is an attempt to make basic theological knowledge easily understood for the general population, including those outside of the church and Christianity. It is vital that basic theological knowledge be packaged for dissemination to the general public. One of the aims of this book is to begin the process or contribute to the process of overcoming the theological/biblical knowledge deficit in the society and in the world.

It is acknowledged that theological knowledge is voluminous and no one can master all of it. The aim of this book is to present some foundational principles of theology and core biblical truths that are relevant and vital for human survival. There is an urgency to overcoming the theological knowledge deficit to prevent an impending global technological catastrophe. The world has become too dangerous for our leaders and citizens to be theologically uninformed. It is a compounded tragedy to perish for a lack of knowledge.

It is tragic because the knowledge and blue print for human survival is available. It has been available for over 2000 years. It is the urgent challenge of theology and theologians to decipher the core values and the primary salvation message of religion to be instilled in religious, educational, industrial, cultural and social institutions. It is a must that leaders embrace the core values of true religion, theological knowledge and the highest and most sound ethical and moral values.

Mass media, propelled by advance information technology, bombards society daily with the crime problem, the political, economic and social problems. Since we are inundated daily with the social and cultural crises, it would be superfluous and redundant to dwell on the problems and crises. Therefore, this literary work will be devoted to defining the meaning and the critical role of public theology in a nation and a society that is going down the immoral, unethical and idolatrous slippery slope of no return.

The premises, inferences, assumptions and principles of this book can be verified by theological study and the authoritative biblical truth of the Holy Bible. It is my hope that this book will generate more interest in the study of theology and the Bible as well as consultation with those who are knowledgeable of God's Word. It is my hope that persons who want to know more about God's Word and God's Will, will feel free to consult with knowledgeable Christians, join fellowships and Bible classes as well as establish fellowship groups and Bible study groups in and out of the church. It goes without saying that increased knowledge and understanding of the Bible will bring about increased knowledge and understanding of public theology. Most, if not all of the premises set forth in this book will be self evident and will not require the additions of references and footnotes.

One major premise of this book is that God has set the standards for all human relationships in God's divine law and his natural laws. God has set the standards for human conduct and human covenants and relationships. The second premise that is assumed under the first premise is that when God's standards (laws) are violated the consequences are detrimental to the human enterprise. These premises are so self-evident that it would be superfluous to enumerate and document the evidence. However, for those who want the evidence, I suggest that they study the Bible, listen to and look at the daily news. You will find them replete with violations and consequences.

Statutory laws are manmade laws. They can be changed, eliminated and re-written. Statutory laws can be in congruence with divine law and natural law or in conflict with them. Statutory manmade laws cannot change the divine laws and natural laws made by God. When statutory laws go against the divine laws of God as revealed in the Holy Bible and the natural laws in nature, they become contrary to God's Will and the natural order of the universe. The consequence of such contrary laws become transgressive perversions that are doomed for failure and destruction.

Laws and behavior that are contrary to God's Will are damaging and destructive to society and humanity as a whole. Therefore, it is the responsibility of civilized, representative government to eliminate and prohibit the establishment of laws that would allow and sanction behavior and policies that go against divine law, natural law and valid congruent statutory laws. Divine laws and natural laws are based on the truth, justice, sound doctrine and the righteousness of God. In the making of statutory laws, theology can determine whether those statutory laws are in congruence with divine law and natural law.

Manmade laws and human judicial decisions are often arbitrary, relative, opinionated and even biased. It is commonplace to witness split decisions by the U. S. Supreme Court with five to four margins that could go either way. It is clear that legal decisions are not always right, just or good decisions. Therefore, statutory law is open to the sanction and the validation of wrong, unnatural and unjust legal decisions. Also, the wide latitude of judicial discretion that judges have, allows for arbitrary judicial decisions and abuse of authority. It must be noted that arbitrary decisions and abuse of authority is not limited to judges or the judicial system. It happens at every level of society. Public theology can play a major and significant role in reducing and eliminating harmful arbitrary and capricious decisions.

Public theology provides a transcendent dimension above political science, government and culture. Theology has validated divine revelatory knowledge and moral laws that supersede manmade laws and ordinary human knowledge. There is an urgency that this theological knowledge be made public in every arena of life and especially among leaders. Since this knowledge has been available for over two thousand years, one may raise the question, "Why must this vital theological knowledge be applied with such urgency?" The answer is obvious and simple: For the first time in the history of civilization, humanity is living on the brink of disaster.

Public theology is inclusive of ethics, morality, mercy love and the Will of God. Theology is knowledgeable of the standards set by God. Theology knows that humanity is at the mercy of God. Human culture cannot solve itself. The increased knowledge and the increased sophistication of technology have increased the possibility of humankind self-destruction. Therefore, the answer is not found in secular knowledge or the scientific technology. Secular knowledge and secular technology empower man's ability to self-destruct.

It is the transcendent dimensions of theology that declares that human life and the soul of man are supreme sacred values that reflect the image and likeness of God. Human life and the human soul must be reverenced with the utmost respect. Jesus declared, "Verily I say unto you, inasmuch as ye have done it unto one of the least of these my brethren, ye have done it unto me." (Matthew 25:40, KJV). Theology declares that degradations and violations of human life are offensive to God and are in opposition to God's Will. Theology knows that if the ills of the world are to be corrected and healed there must be a primacy of respect and love for human life from the womb to the tomb.

Theology has documented historically that the Holy Bible has the longest continuity of divine revelatory knowledge than any other volume in history. This record of divine revelation covers a historical period of more than four thousand years. It reveals

God's intention and God's progressive self-disclosure in human history. It is a progressive revelation because theology has traced its development from its beginning, genesis, development, growth, completion and culmination in the fulfillment of Jesus Christ. Jesus Christ is the fulfillment of the beginning, the development, growth and the completion of the Bible. Therefore, the understanding and the interpretation of all scripture must be done in the light of Jesus Christ and his Gospel. Jesus Christ, the mind of Christ and the Holy Spirit are the final authority and interpreter of scripture and truth.

The Bible must be judged as a whole. It must be judged by its beginning, progressive development and culmination in Jesus Christ. It cannot be rightly, adequately or validly judged on the basis of any singular parts or persons included among and in its 66 Books. It must be judged by its Alpha and Omega.

If the Holy Bible is not the validated universal authority for humanity, what is that validated authority? If Jesus Christ is not the validated way, truth and life for humanity, who is the validated way, truth and life for humanity? If there is another name other than Jesus Christ given among men whereby we must be saved, name the name.

The <u>Principles and Practice of Public Theology</u> is a guide for implementing God's salvation plan for this world. This plan is a part of God's divine master plan for humankind. This plan is biblically based in Christian theology. This is a clear practical plan based on God's Word, common sense, common logic, reasonable rationality, compassion and the Will of God. It is mandated and authorized by God. It teaches, equips, guides and gives meaning and significance to all salvation plans of benevolence and goodwill. It is a comprehensive and inclusive plan.

This plan includes the benevolent and divine use of science, art and religion. It includes the private and public. It includes educational institutions, business and industry. It includes all races, cultures, nationalities and humanity. It is based on the revealed knowledge from God above. This divine knowledge comes from beyond human culture to save human culture and human souls.

What is this plan and how can it be implemented? The plan is to use the knowledge of God to do the Will of God. Theology has sufficient knowledge and principles of God to determine the Will of God. The guiding principles for the Will of God are truth, justice, goodness, righteousness, mercy, love, benevolence, goodwill, wisdom, knowledge, understanding and the Holy Spirit. These principles can be taught and applied in every human situation. The adherence to, and the application of, these principles constitute the Will of God. These principles can be applied in every situation by all people everywhere.

The living principles and attributes of God consist of the vertical dimension from God. Another way of expressing the vertical dimension, which is the channel from God to humanity, is the theological perspective. The theological perspective is that perspective or view from the Will of God. The theological perspective can be applied in every human situation. The theological perspective is a consult with the Will or Spirit of God. The theological consult requests God's Will, God's way, God's wisdom, God's understanding and God's guidance in all decisions and actions.

This request of God's Will is utilized through seeking God's Will through the vertical theological perspectives found in the divine ethical principles provided by God. The principles of righteousness, justice and love are based on true and sound doctrine. In every imaginable human situation a theological perspective can be applied. The application of the theological perspective is the right, ethical, moral and pro-life decision. The theological perspective provides an opportunity for an enlightened right and best rational and ethical decision.

Human decisions and actions void of the theological perspective run the risk of being haphazard, random and arbitrary. Arbitrary decisions are often misguided and unethical and subsequently, wreak tragic consequences. Decisions and actions void of theological consult and perspective are unenlightened and lack moral authority. The margin of error in decision-making and actions must be minimized to reduce costly mistakes and human suffering. Bad decisions usually result in bad consequences. The theological perspective offers an opportunity to make good rational intelligent decisions.

The convergence of diverse cultures, religions, races, ethnicities and nationalities coupled with technological capabilities, makes it mandatory to adopt the theological perspective decision-making approach.

As the society becomes more complex, the decision-making must become more accurate. The hope for that increased accuracy lies in the vertical dimension of public theology and the theological perspective.

The biblical mandates have always required the theological perspective in decision-making and actions. The associated complexities of modern technological society has ushered in the urgency of the biblical mandates of the theological perspective. It is clear that the social sciences, natural sciences and government bureaucracies do not have the answers to face the challenges of the ongoing threatening culture crises in the world of the 21st century.

Therefore, the theological perspective, which has always been with humankind, must now be asserted with urgency and full force. This vertical dimensional message from God must be spread horizontally to all people through the leadership of public theology. Since theological knowledge is so scarce and limited in the public and private sector, there must be a vigorous reinforcement in the education and training of public theologians. Theological training must be geared towards practical applications in all areas of society. The practice of public theology must be expanded beyond the traditional roles of theology, which has been primarily in the church. It must be expanded to educational institutions, business and other industrial enterprises.

Public theology is the challenging new outpost for the church. It is the institution of the church that must put forth the leadership in the training and practice of public theology. The crises and turmoils in the society are threatening to overwhelm society and the church. The church is that institution which is connected with the theological perspective from God. Therefore, the church must expand and accelerate its mission and broaden its ministerial horizons.

This book is written to give focus, direction and reinforcement to the public theology movement. It is written to enhance the building of strong public theological institutions to specialize in the training and the practice of the primary survival theological principles for the human family. Through the validated sound doctrines of truth, a healthier culture and a more congenial sanctuary for the human spirit can be reconstructed in the global society. The public theology movement will give the church a challenge and an opportunity to share outside of its walls, the salvation knowledge of Jesus Christ and to unleash its spiritual citadel of faith, hope and love.

In an effort to provide continuous support for the public theology movement, two organizations were incorporated through the state of Georgia in September and October 2002 respectively. The first not-for-profit organization is the Christian Institute of Public Theology. This organization is incorporated to provide education, training and service for public theology. The second not-for-profit organization is the Christian Association of Public Theologians. This is a fellowship and membership organization to carry out the mission of public theology. On September 22 - 23, 2006, the Christian Association of Public Theologians held its first annual conference at the Morehouse School of Medicine in Atlanta, Georgia. Dr. Robert M. Franklin, former president of the Interdenominational Theological Center (ITC) in Atlanta, Georgia was the keynote speaker for the first Christian Association of Public Theologians (CAPT) Conference. Dr. Franklin is a leading advocate for public theology. The initial members of CAPT were my students who graduated from the certificate in theology program through ITC in Atlanta from 2001-2006.

My initial introduction to the concept of public theology was during my undergraduate study in religion at Morehouse College. The Reverend Lucius M. Tobin, my instructor and mentor in religion, taught extensively about the social gospel and the theologians who wrote about and were involved with the social gospel movement, especially in Germany and the United States in the 1940s during and after World War II. The social gospel concepts were fascinating to me because my religious orientation consisted primarily of individual salvation. I had not known about group salvation or institutional salvation prior to my studies under Professor Lucius M. Tobin at Morehouse College. In addition to the concepts of the social gospel, Rev. Tobin expressed his keen insights into the culture crisis. The culture crisis became a theme of Rev. Tobin's teachings in religion. Rev. Tobin felt it was the duty of religion to deal with the culture crisis. Rev. Tobin was my instructor during the early 1960s at Morehouse College.

The concepts of the social gospel and the culture crises remained with me during my work and ministry at the Wheat Street Baptist Church from 1964 to 1990 in Atlanta. During this time I founded an organization in the church's youth department known as the Christian Services Institute. Although this organization became inactive when I left Wheat Street Baptist Church in 1990, it was my organization on paper.

It was during my tenure as a student and later as an instructor at ITC where I adopted the concept of public theology. The concept of public theology incorporated, for me, the concepts of the social gospel and the Christian Services Institute. Public theology conveys the concern of God for the community and a rational religious and spiritual approach for the theological practitioner.

Public theology provides the God connection to the community, as well as the church. The concept of public theology rightly, expands the relevance and the jurisdiction of religion to the whole society.

The Christian public theological focus in this volume is intended to be universally inclusive. The services and the membership participation are open to all persons everywhere. However, Christian public theology is not intended to speak for or negate the significance of public theology in other religions.

There is room for other religions to develop and practice public theology. There is hope for greater understanding and greater good in society through the associations of public theology of other religions. It is hoped that the concept and organizations of public theology will evolve into the International Association of Public Theologians. Such an organization would allow for qualified representatives of all religions to be represented. This would give theology the universal impact that is needed.

This book is the product of a broad variety of sources, persons, ideas, experiences and influences. It reflects all of the internal and external influences of my life. It reflects the feelings ideas and thoughts of my life-long journey. I cannot possibly enumerate all the persons and sources that have touched and influenced my life and thoughts. I can only make mention of a very few in regards to the contents of this book.

My basic concepts of public theology and the practice of public theology evolved from my personal experience and my professional experience in the study and in the practicing roles of ministry. My journey started when I was a child seeking to know God. I joined a Baptist church while a student in elementary school. I became interested in the vertical dimension of religion during my childhood. From that time forth, I was always preoccupied in some form or another with the vertical dimension pathway to God. I felt the hand of God in my life at an early age. I felt the inspiration of God when I delivered the valedictorian address upon graduation from the eighth grade. Three and one half years later while a senior at Tuskegee Institute High School, I was converted and ordained for the ministry. I graduated with honors and a president of my senior class.

My education at Morehouse College in Atlanta, Georgia was significant for many reasons. The renowned educator, theologian and writer, Benjamin Elijah Mays, was president of Morehouse College. The Morehouse School of Religion was also located on the campus of Morehouse College during my tenure. For four years I attended the daily chapel services in Sale Hall on campus. The Reverend Lucius M. Tobin became my professor of religion as well as my religious mentor. It was Rev. Tobin who provided me with the significant connection between public theology and the culture crisis. He felt that it is the duty of religion (public theology) to meet the challenge of the culture crisis. He also felt that the great challenge of religion is to save humanity from the destructive threat of technology and conflicting cultures, races and religions.

Morehouse College provided a significant foundation in my pursuit to understand more about the vertical and horizontal dimensions of the cross that connects man with God and the human with the divine. While at Morehouse I received the Benjamin E. Mays debating prize, the most outstanding student in religion award and was selected to preach the senior sermon in the Morehouse Chapel upon my graduation. All of my experiences, knowledge and education continued to be used to make religion more practical and more relevant for the primary and ultimate needs of the people.

My forty plus years of employment with the government in the secular world has influenced my ideas regarding public theology. I have worked simultaneously in the church as a teacher, preacher, counselor and pastor.

Public theology has been an obsession of mine since I was a child. In my early years I did not know the name for the concept of public theology during the early years. Upon reflection I can see how the concept of public theology evolved in my own thinking, education and experiences. Although I was employed in government agencies for more than forty years to provide criminal justice system services, mental health and substance abuse services, education and administration, I always felt that I was really working for God regardless of the many job titles I have had. The theological dimension and the theological perspective were always my guide and primary motivation. I have worked under many professional titles and certifications, but I was always a minister of Jesus Christ, first and foremost.

In addition to the public theology in my employment, public theology has also been employed in my volunteer community work with numerous councils and boards I participated in and held positions. I was the president of my community association for twenty years. I lived in a neighborhood where over 90 percent of the residents went to the polls and voted. I consider working for the Kingdom of God in Jesus Christ in the public or private domain as public theology.

I have provided the preceding experiential enumerations to highlight the practicality of public theology and to give credence to this volume. Public theology is not a mystical or complex concept. It is the practical work of God in the service to humanity throughout the community and society. There are countless numbers of public theologians. Now that the concept is clarified, the challenge is to advocate for public theology, recruit and train more public theologians for more effective theologically oriented service to the community.

There is a need for public theological institutions to develop special educational curricula for the education and training of public theologians for the challenges of the twenty first century. I would be remiss if I did not acknowledge my M.A. degree from Clark Atlanta University in Sociology, the M. S. degree from Georgia State University in Public Policy and Administration, and the Master of Divinity degree from the Morehouse School of Religion at ITC in Atlanta, Georgia as being valuable education for public theology. However, if it were not for my knowledge of the Holy Bible and personal salvation knowledge in Jesus Christ all of my other knowledge and experiences would be for naught.

I learned the significance of public theology through my own work experiences. In my long years of employment in the world of work, I have worked in many positions. I was blessed with success as a probation officer supervisor, project director correction specialist, court referee hearing officer, probation parole supervisor, criminal justice coordinator, forensic counselor, EAP specialist, equal employment opportunity and affirmative action officer, mental health professional supervisor, theological instructor and other associated positions. However, the point I want to make about these various positions is that they were all ministries for me. I was successful in all of my positions because I considered myself as working for God. I received the Georgia Governor's Award in 1987 for establishing mental health and substance abuse services in the criminal justice systems.

The significant thing that I discovered in my work experiences was that I would not have experienced the level of success that I did, had it not been for the theological factors operating in my life. After reflecting on and evaluating my forty-year work career, I came to the conclusion that the theological perspective made a positive difference. This is what has convinced me that theology and the theological perspective and involvement is needed in the public domain as well as in the private church and Christian institutions. Theology is not merely needed in the public domain; it belongs in the public domain. An acute urgency in our growing social problems and culture crises demand the employment of public theology in every phase of our private and public lives. Public theology simply means that individuals and groups must begin to utilize sound doctrines and true values in their decisions and in their actions. We can no longer ignore ethical values given by God as guides for our lives. When we ignore the ethical standards set by God, we jeopardize ourselves, our souls and conditions for the existence of the human enterprise. Great damage has already been done to humanity as a whole, as well as to the earthly habitation for the existence of life.

The theological perspective offers a way back from the dark abyss we face. It offers the way out of darkness. The theological perspective is available. It has been my guide in my work in the secular world. It is the way that acknowledges God, reverences life, the way of righteousness, truth, justice, compassion and the common good. Theology is the means of connecting with the Will and ways of God in our decisions and in our actions and relationships.

It is the challenge, responsibility and duty for every human individual and every human group to choose the superior way and Will of God in all that we say and do. In every legitimate job, positions or endeavor, we must perceive ourselves as serving humanity according to the Will and ways of God. Builders and engineers who serve humanity under God build more secure structures. Vehicle drivers who consider the sacredness of life observe the optimum in safety. Counselors, administrators and other human service providers maintain competence, compassion and ethics because they respect the sacredness and dignity of human life. Custodians and maintenance personnel who are servants of God take a special pride in their work. Food that is prepared, cooked and served by public theologians (or public Christians) is more healthy, tasty and safer for consumption. Police officers who are public theologians are trustworthier as they seek to protect the rights, persons and property of citizens and persons in the community. I would be very skeptical of a police officer who is armed and entrusted to protect the rights of others who does not have a theological perspective. How can any public servant be trusted by the people if they do not have loyalty to God and a code of ethics of righteousness and honesty? Public theology is on solid ground when it advocates that persons who serve the public possess a bona fide benevolent loyalty to God.

School teachers who adopt the theological perspective will not only transmit valuable academic knowledge, but will also pass on spiritual values, character development and a concern for the common good. The school system has the greatest opportunity for transforming the culture and society. Because there are more full time and prime time teachers of impressionable youth in the schools of greater periods of time than there are in any other institution. When school systems and schoolteachers adopt the theological perspective and become redemptively involved in the educational process, rapid and massive changes will take place for good in our society.

The ideas contained in this book evolved through all of my associations and social situations from as far back as I can remember. Therefore, I am indebted to all persons, agencies, groups and institutions that have touched my life and entered my thoughts. I wish to acknowledge Macedonia Baptist Church where I was baptized, licensed and ordained to preach the Gospel; my graduation from Tuskegee Institute High School; Board member of Alabama Bible University in Notasulga, Alabama. I wish to express gratitude for serving in the pulpit under the pastorate of the Reverend William Holmes Borders, Sr. for twenty years. Thanks to the staff members and residents of the Foundation Baptist Church at Summerset Assistant Living Community in Atlanta. Thanks to the pastor and members of Calvary Baptist Church, which hosted the first ITC, classes that I taught in Atlanta.

Expressions of gratitude to Pastor Hoke L. Smith and Calvary Baptist Church for hosting the first meeting of the Christian Association of Public Theology in Madison, Georgia.

Pastor James H. Sims, Jr., of the Shiloh Missionary Baptist Church in Atlanta, has provided indispensable support for the ITC Certificate in Theology program along with the Christian Association of Public Theologians. Reverend Sims and Shiloh also hosted the first theological courses provided through the Christian Institute of Public Theology.

I wish to commend the Reverend Carl Dickerson, assistant to Reverend Sims, who has been faithful and consistent in his accommodations and stewardship of the educational and church building for the many activities held at Shiloh. I wish to thank Madge D. Owens for typing this manuscript and getting it in acceptable form for publication. Thanks to all of my students and the public theologians who are preparing to provide leadership for the public theology movement. Thanks to Wilma and Karen, my wife and daughter, who allowed me the time and space to do this writing.

Thanks be to God for His mercy and the guidance of His Holy Spirit in Christ.

Chapter 2

The Vision for Public Theology

The vision for public theology is to provide for humanity, the vital leadership for reaching and actualizing the benevolent God gifted potential for good for the human race. This vision inspires the optimum aspiration of the soul. It is the human up reach and the human uplift to God. It is intended and designed to raise humanity to the lofty heights intended by God.

Through the leadership of public theology, the science of ethics, the intelligence of morality, emotional maturity, social refinement, cultural enrichment and spiritual enlightenment can be realized. These realizations can be translated into the institutionalization and institutional practice of those sentiments, values and behaviors that are good, true, beautiful and righteous. Theology has at its disposal an inexhaustible resource of knowledge, skills and values that can be taught and disseminated throughout society. There is a great hunger and a vital need for this theological knowledge. Humanity is perishing for lack of knowledge.

Let it be known that this life and soul saving knowledge is available. The challenge of public theology is to make this knowledge known, relevant and practical for the benefit of society and for the salvation of humankind.

The anointed theologian is given the authority and the insight to look beyond what exists naturally, and declare what ought to be or should exist spiritually, according to the intended Will of God.

The anointed theologian is in touch with the knowledge and power to transform what is into what ought to be. Natural discernment can describe what is; but it is through theological spiritual enlightenment that affirms what ought to be according to the manifested Will of God. It is the duty and domain of theology to provide the ethical, right, moral and equitable decision in all human situations. It is the theological perspective that gives balance, unity and coherence to all other perspectives. It is the theological perspective that is able to view the whole from all dimensions.

The theological perspective is that overall comprehensive perspective that under girds, surrounds and formulates the congruence for all the other perspectives. It is essential for the theological perspective to be holistic in order to make accurate judgments and right decisions. The human situation and the social situation involve a multiplicity of components and perspectives. In every human and social situation, there will be sociological, psychological, physiological, biological and anthropological perspectives. In addition to these perspectives, there are often other components, such as the legal, political, economic, historical, and so forth.

The foregoing perspectives and components were mentioned in order to illustrate more clearly, the unique role of the theological perspective. All of the named perspectives and components exist on the horizontal dimension except for the theological perspective.

The theological perspective is the only one that claims a connection with the vertical dimension. It is the only one that makes the connection between God and man; therefore, the theological perspective is not just one of many perspectives regarding the human and socialization. It is that perspective that under girds, surrounds and formulates the congruence for the other perspectives and components. The theological perspective is the one that provides the essence and the ultimate meaning and significance of the other perspectives and the social units that they form.

It is the theological perspective that provides unity, harmony, integration, guidance, meaning and significance to the other components and perspectives. The theological perspective is operational on all human levels. It can be applied to individuals, couples, and groups. It can be applied to all human entities, such as schools, businesses, governing bodies, cities, states and nations, races and ethnicities. The theological perspective is international and universal. It acknowledges the jurisdiction and the Will of God over all individuals, all groups of individuals and nature itself.

The theological perspective is a major theme of this work. Therefore, it will be treated with more specificity and details. The references that are made to God's Will are not meant to be viewed in a mystical or abstract sense. It is not meant to be viewed in a psychic or intuitive way. The theological perspective is reality based. It arrives at the Will of God through the reality based concrete social situation by way of the facts, the truth and the presenting set of circumstances. The challenge of this work is to make the theological perspective so simple, common and practical that people everywhere will adopt it and use it for the betterment of themselves and for the common good.

Willie James Webb

Chapter 3

The Theological Perspective

The theological perspective can be applied in every human situation. The purpose of this book is to show the critical importance of applying the theological perspective in all human situations, and notions about what that perspective is. The theological perspective is already being applied by many persons. It may not be recognized as such and it may not be done consistently. Hopefully, this volume will describe what the theological perspective is, and the vital necessity of applying it broadly and consistently.

The theological perspective is the application of the Will of God in all human situations. It is the employment of the revealed transcendent knowledge of God's Will. This transcendent knowledge refers primarily to the true knowledge as recorded in the Old Testament and the New Testament of the Holy Bible. The cross is an illustration of the dimension of this knowledge. The cross has a vertical and horizontal dimension. The vertical dimension of the cross represents the up reach to God. It also represents the disclosure of the revelation of God from above to human beings below. The horizontal dimension of the cross represents the outreach of human beings to each other. The cross symbolizes man's discovery from beneath and God's revelation from above.

The theological perspective incorporates the Will of God in all human affairs. This perspective is not new. It is an old perspective. Jesus says in the Lord's Prayer, "Thy Kingdom come, Thy Will be done, on earth, as it is in heaven." It is very clear that the Will of God must become the Will of the believers in God. This being self evident, it is incumbent upon the believers of God to place a top priority on finding out what God's Will is for our individual lives, as well as for our corporate lives.

God's Will is based on very concrete established principles, instructions and guidelines. God has established a universal moral order with distinctions between what is good and evil, and what is right and wrong. The choices of good and right are in line with the Will of God. God has created a scale of balance, which determines that which is just and that which is unjust. Behaviors and decisions that are just and equitable are in line with the Will of God. Just decisions help to maintain balance in human equations and thereby minimize conflict and increase the prospect for peace.

In addition to establishing a moral order in the universe, God has also created moral values. Moral values are positive and benevolent values. They consist of that which is good, true, right and beautiful. Moral values enhance, nurtures and support human life. The Golden Rule, the Ten Commandments and the Hippocratic Oath are examples of moral values. Observing and upholding moral values are in line with the Will of God. This is an indication as to how broadly the theological perspective can be applied.

The theological perspective prioritizes the corporate good or the common good of the whole body. This theological perspective is so important that Jesus stated that if the hand or the eye become offensive to the body, they must be cut off and plucked out to save the body. Working for and protecting the common good of the whole body is in line with the Will of God. A theological perspective that works for the good of humanity and civilization are in line with the Will of God. It only takes common sense and common logic to see the importance and the wisdom in working for the common good. If individuals fail to work for the common good, there will be no security for the individual good. Therefore, theology must expand its domain to the public and common good. In a growing fragmenting self-centered society, it is urgent that a renewed emphasis must be placed on cultivating the common good.

The theological perspective consists of transcendent knowledge of God conscious decisions with spiritual enlightenment and ethical awareness for the common good of humanity. In every human situation a theological construct can be formed to make the right decision or take the right position. The vertical dimension from God provides upon consultation the right answers and the just solutions when they are seen or approached from the theological perspective. This theological perspective comes about through seeking and asking for the truth and for understanding and guidance.

If we honestly look, it is not so difficult to see that which is right, that which is good, that which is just and that which is in the best interest of human life and the common good. When an individual becomes knowledgeable with the scriptures of the Holy Bible and the saving grace of Jesus Christ, it is easy to see that which is good, true, beautiful and merciful because they are illuminated by the light and life of Christ.

It is acknowledged that there are complex problems and social situations that defy simple answers and solutions. The new technology and cultural diversity and religious pluralism present more challenging questions and solutions. However, the updated and evolving theological perspective in Jesus Christ has the answers and solutions for the new challenges. In Christ, we have the truth, resurrection, salvation, grace and unconditional love. The question is raised, "How can the new problems of technology and social dynamic changes be answered in a theological perspective?"

Most, if not all, of society's social and technological problems can be solved by doing that which is right, just, moral, ethical and that which is in the best interest of the common good.

The ethical, moral and spiritual teachings of the Holy Bible make the claim of being the message of God for all people for all times. In spite of the advances of modern civilization and modern technology, human nature remains the same. Man cannot get away from his human nature and his need for God and God's guidance and prescription for his human nature. Therefore, the theological perspective and the theological prescription will always be relevant for man's success and survival in his mortal human predicament.

The messages of laws, prophecies, promises and proverbs of the Old Testament evolved and culminated into the fulfillment of love, grace and truth in Jesus Christ. Therefore, the final authority and interpreter of Scripture is Jesus Christ. Jesus is the way, the truth, the life and the standard set by God. It is the mind of Christ through the enlightenment of the Holy Spirit that is the ultimate theological perspective. It is through the mind of Christ that Godly decisions, right decisions, just decisions, ethical decisions, moral decisions, merciful decisions and loving decisions can be made. "Let this mind be in you, which was also in Christ Jesus." (Philippians 2:5, KJV)

CHAPTER 4

What Is Public Theology?

Public theology is the benevolent and redemptive engagement of a rational and purpose driven religious expression for human salvation and for the common good of society. It is a rational organized effort to employ the resources of God to persuade and influence human beings to embrace those principles of God that are designed for mankind's optimum fulfillment and ultimate salvation. Public theology connotes scientific, artistic, aesthetic, religious, ethical and spiritual knowledge that makes known the nature, will, power, works, ways, wisdom spirit and love of God to and for all humanity.

Public theology consists of individually and socially redemptive expressions and activities designed for the common good of all people. It seeks to analyze and synthesize social events and social situations to determine what is the most positive option and loving decision that ought to be made according to God's Will and purpose for humanity. Public theology is the injection of the vertical dimension of religion that connects God to human beings and human affairs. This God and human connection is recorded in the Holy Bible. It has been authoritatively demonstrated and validated by the life and teachings of Jesus Christ. God's laws of living and love in Jesus Christ reigns supreme.

Public theology is concerned with ethical balance, congruence and equity in human affairs and in human relationships. Public theology places an emphasis on the rational and intellectual side of religion. It utilizes objectivity, rational reflection, factual knowledge, manifested evidences, and observable realities in the theory and practice of religion. It seeks to harmonize and optimize emotional fervor with rational analysis in the light of existing realities. It seeks to use strong feelings to energize positive and redemptive actions. The intellect and the emotions work together more effectively when the emotions provide the driving force and the rational enlightened mind provide the guiding force. The autonomous mind is capable of making decisions, choosing options and determining directions and priorities. The mind that is infused with public theological knowledge and motivated by a heart of love is capable of analyzing social situations and navigating through social complexities and arriving at equitable and righteous decisions.

Since we have alluded to the notion that public theology is a guidance system for humanity, we are obligated to make clear what that guidance system is ultimately. The question naturally arises as to how can there be a predetermined guidance system when society is in flux and social situations are constantly changing. Biblical truth is made for human nature and humankind. The redemptive salvation teaching and sacrificial love of Jesus Christ are relevant for all ages. The divine truth and unconditional love of God never become outdated. In addition to the continuing relevance of God's word, God became intimately personalized in Jesus Christ. Therefore, through identifying with Jesus Christ, public theology translates into seeing, hearing, understanding, witnessing and interpreting social situations and events according to the mind of Christ. The Christian public theologian has the mind of Christ as the ultimate guide.

The mind of Christ knows what ought to be as opposed to what is. It is the mind of Christ that reveals the right way in the midst of multiple ways; the truth in the mix of errors; life in the presence of death. It is the mind of Christ that sheds light, wisdom and understanding in every individual and social situation. It is the mind of Christ that sees, hears and reveals God's Will, even in dynamic and changing social situations. Jesus is that stability which underlies the transitory processes of human interactions. He is the righteousness of God. He is the divine standard for measuring that, which is morally, ethically and spiritually true, good and righteous in all human affairs.

In contrast to the concept of religion, the concept of public theology places an emphasis on specialized knowledge of religion to be utilized with a rational expertise for the public good. Religion in general has innumerable ways of expressing itself. The most common known expressions of religion are found in the worship and ministerial activities of the church. Worship services in most of the churches are characterized by meditation, singing, praying, preaching, rituals and ceremonial services.

Emotionalism plays a major role in the worship services of many, if not most of the churches. This is not a bad thing. It serves a beneficial purpose for most of the parishioners because emotional expressions in the church can be therapeutic. However, this vast magnitude of emotionalism is not necessarily translated into or focused on public theology.

Church worship services can easily (though unintentionally) become exclusive and private affairs. The church is often effective in its fellowship and services for its members. The church fellowship can easily become withdrawn from the general society and from the outside world of reality. In contrast to the general and traditional way in which the church operates, public theology is designed to transmit the values, knowledge, requirements and benefits of the word and the Will of God to the public sector of society. Public theology is an extension of the church and the services of the church to the broad society. Therefore, every church has a responsibility for the practice of public theology.

The church has a primary responsibility for public theology because the church is the primary guardian of the revelation and message of God. The church has the responsibility to get that message outside of its walls and into every sector of society. The authorization message of Jesus Christ commissions his disciples and Christian believers to go into all the world. The commission of Jesus includes preaching and teaching the Gospel, feeding hungry minds, souls and bodies, healing the broken hearted, giving sight to the blind, preaching deliverance to the captives, to set at liberty those that are bruised and in bondage, shine the light of Christ for those in darkness.

Getting the message and establishing the message in the public domain is not a simple task. It is an awesome challenge for the church. The challenge is awesome because there is a growing and strong resistance against the message of God in public. It is also challenging because education and training will be required by the church if the effort is to be effective and successful. Public theology is the most vital and urgent need for a theologically uninformed and misguided society in the 21st Century. Public theology incorporates scientific knowledge and all recognized valid bodies of knowledge. Public theology is broad in its focus and scope because its goal is not limited to individual spiritual salvation. It seeks the individual, social, cultural and spiritual redemption of the whole person and the whole society.

How can public theology be applied so broadly and keep its distinction as public theology? It is because theology is uniquely different from all of the other academic disciplines. Theology has a dimension of vertical up reach to God, as well as the horizontal outreach to mankind. All of the other disciplines operate on the horizontal plane. The natural and social sciences operate on the horizontal level. Even astronomy operates on the horizontal level because astronomy studies the phenomenon of nature. The stars are up, but they are a part of nature. All nature is studied on the horizontal level. Theological up is different from scientific, physical or geographical up. The theological up is up to God. It is an up that is beyond nature. God is beyond nature. The spiritual and divine up is different from the physical and human up. Theology makes the claim of a vertical up reach from man to God. Theology reflects on a relationship between God and man, as well as a relationship between God and God's creation.

Public theology can be applied broadly throughout society because of God's sovereignty over man and creation. There are no off limits to God in God's universe. Theology acknowledges the absolute jurisdiction of God as being over everything, including the creatures and the creation. There is a theological perspective that can be added to every situation and circumstance. It is the duty of public theology to construct the theological perspective to every situation. This theological perspective is designed to yield the best outcome, the right outcome, the just outcome. Theological perspective is designed to say or declare what ought to be according to the Will and wisdom of God. It is the choice of what is godly, redemptive, loving and that, which is in the best interest of the common good.

Important and even vital decisions are made daily in the home, in business, education, health, government institutions and even in the church without a theological consult. Too often, there is no moral, ethical or God consciousness in the day-by-day life choices and decision-making of most people. How tragic it must be when individuals make inferior (less than best) and arbitrary decisions without considering the Will of God and what is best for the common good. This tragedy is compounded when individuals make ungodly and arbitrary decisions for other people. This speaks to persons who are in leadership and authoritative positions. It ranges from parents who make decisions for their children, principals for schools, managers for jobs, directors of corporations, pastors of churches, officials of government, military commanders and the president of nations. Decision-making determines life and death, success and failures, blessings and curses.

Therefore, it must be resolved that competent, enlightened, ethical and right decision-making receives top priority from top to bottom in every situation throughout the society.

Ultimately, ethical and moral decisions derive from the vertical dimension of religion.

The premise of public theology is based on the universal symbol of the cross. The vertical dimension of the cross represents the up reach to God. The horizontal dimension of the cross is the outreach to the neighbors, sisters and brothers. This horizontal outreach extends beyond the self, the family and beyond the walls of the church, beyond cultures, governments, races and nationalities. The horizontal outreach is as broad as humanity. The vertical up reach is above humanity. However, it is connected to humanity.

The cross represents the unique connection and the unique relationship between God and man. It is a touching and connecting relationship. It represents the intersection of time and eternity, the human and the divine. It represents an intervention in history by a power beyond history. This power beyond history has become accessible and disclosed in history. This power is focused on the salvation of mankind. It is the duty of public theology to make this power known to humanity everywhere. The cross represents God's agonizing concern for humanity. It represents the suffering and sacrifice for humanity. It is the supreme sacrifice from above. It was a public sacrifice on Mount Calvary.

The cross at Calvary represents victory and triumph. It represents goodness overcoming evil and the light overcoming the darkness. It is a victory of righteousness over wrong and justice over injustice. The cross at Calvary validates the truth and vindicates the righteousness of God through the resurrection of Jesus Christ. The cross at Calvary answers the age-old question: "If a man dies, can he live again?" Death was defeated at the cross. Jesus offers hope and the only hope for eternal life. Considering the magnitude of escalating world crises, the ethics and teachings of Jesus Christ offer the only hope for the survival of civilization. The public theologians must accept the responsibility of getting the message of Jesus Christ to the public sectors of the world. The salvation and survival message is available, but is concealed and privatized by Christians who have conformed to the comforts of this world.

The Gospel is not just vital for spiritual salvation beyond this earthly life. The Gospel is also vital for personal, social and cultural salvation in this present life on the earth. The Gospel offers the best plan for human survival. I venture to say that it is the only workable plan for human survival. It is vital that this plan be made known and implemented with urgency. Public theology is the serious strategically redemptive engagement of the most enlightened benevolent religious thought and practice with the whole society.

Public Theology is that academic discipline that studies and makes known the nature of God, Will of God, power of God, works of God, spirit of God, ways of God to all humanity. Unlike other academic disciplines, public theology is based on God's creation and God's special revelation in history. Theology has a focus on the relationship between God and mankind in history. History is emphasized because the Holy Bible is a historical document that records the intervention and the actions of God in human history.

Theology accepts and recognizes the absoluteness and total sovereignty of God. Public theology based on the authority of Jesus Christ, extends the revelatory witness of God beyond the walls and the private fellowships out into the public domain. It is the responsibility of the believers in God to express the Will of God and the demonstrated acts of God in all human affairs.

Public theology arises and is resurrected at this juncture in human history due to an acute crisis in the global human culture. That acute culture crisis is that the potential destructiveness made possible by scientific technology has advanced beyond human morality and civility to control and contain it. The lethal power of technology is escalating, while the moral and ethical conduct of humanity is deteriorating. The overall human morality and compassionate concern for the common good has stagnated and degenerated at a time in history when we can least afford. Based on the available knowledge, it is safe to say that the overall culture has been overly saturated with ignorance, evil, immaturity, irresponsibility, greed, immorality, and corruption. The escalating antichrist spirit, disobedience and rebellion against God are root causes of the precarious human predicament.

What is the urgent and practical significance of public theology at this time in history? Public theology is the acknowledgement of God's power and God's Will in all human affairs. It is vital that humanity knows the Will of God for each individual and for humanity in general. God's Will for humanity is redemption and salvation. God gave each individual the freedom to choose between good and evil and between right and wrong. When individuals, groups and nations choose that which is good and do that which is right, they are in congruence with God's Will. As far back as we can trace human history mankind has always known what is good and what is right. This sense of right and wrong, and good and evil were inherently built into human beings. God's goodness and righteousness are guides for human beings to follow.

In the latter days God has made his Will known with unmistakable clarity in the Holy Bible and the life and teachings of

Jesus Christ. Additionally, God lets us know the consequences of our evil and unrighteousness. Unrighteousness and disobedience to God's laws and commandments lead to destruction for individuals, as well as societies and nations.

God is merciful and forgiving; however, unrepentant behavior and continuous disobedience, inevitably leads to destruction. There is ample evidence in the beginning of this 21st century that there is ongoing and continuous disobedience to God's commandments, as well as rejection of Jesus Christ. This disobedience to God and the rejection of Jesus Christ has put society on conflicting collision courses. The clear directions given by God on how to live and follow God's laws have been ignored on a wide scale. This is why society is at great risk for self-destruction.

It seems that God created beings to live according to God's Will. Also, it seems that God designed the world to operate according to God's Will. Things do not go well when they violate the Will of God. It appears that the more God's Will is violated the more dysfunctional and dangerous the society becomes. As we embark upon this 21st century, we are witnessing unprecedented conflicts and dangers. If the world has gone wrong because of the violation of God's Will, it is reasonable to believe that the answer is to get right with God. It is reasonable to believe that if humanity follows God's direction to get in the right relationship with God through Jesus Christ, that there is hope for healing and reconciliation.

There are those who believe that they are individually saved in Christ and regardless of what happens in the world that they will be all right because their individual salvation is assured. Many persons who feel this way are not inclined to be concerned about the common good or the good of the general society. This is an example of private Christianity. Public theology is an effort to get Christians to become public Christians. It is the duty and challenge of Christians to get the message of Jesus Christ into the public domain. It is not necessary to have any theological credentials to be a public Christian. The calling of Christ has always been a public call, a national and universal call. The Gospel of Christ is meant to be shared and spread abroad. However, it is very important to know about God's word, ways, wisdom, works, and love as they are recorded in the Holy Bible.

Public theology is that body of spiritually enlightened knowledge from God to be used for the purpose of making more precise decisions according to the Will of God. The growing complexity of human problems requires more accuracy in their resolution than in the past. Due to the tragic consequences of incompetence and miscalculations, society can no longer afford arbitrary and random solutions to problems. Bad decisions and wrong choices can make bad matters worse. It is the role of public theology to determine what is right and best according to God's Will. In the 21st century it is critical that decisions be made in light of what is right, good, just and in the best interest of society. This is not an advocacy for exclusive theological decisions. It is an advocacy for the inclusion of theological input in decisions that affect the specific and general welfare of society. It is unfortunate that at this time in history, theological input in decisions that affect the specific and general welfare of society is left out. It is unfortunate that at this time in history, theological input and consultation are mostly excluded from the major decisions that affect the general welfare.

There are twelve critical areas where public theological guidance and input is urgently needed as we consider one world, one God and one human family. Serious crises are associated with each of the twelve critical areas:

1. <u>Conflicting Laws and Judicial Decisions</u>
There are volumes and volumes of conflicting laws, locally, nationally and internationally. In one nation and one world, how can arbitrary and conflicting laws be resolved?

2. <u>Forms of Government</u>
What is the right and most equitable form of government? Who authorizes government and who has the legitimate right to govern?

3. <u>Religious Pluralism and Democracy</u>

How can a religion be validated as true or false? How can conflicts in religion and ideologies be resolved?

4. <u>Economic Consumption</u>
There is great disparity in the acquisition and consumption of economic resources. How can more equity and balance be achieved in the acquisition and consumption of economic resources?

5. <u>Stewardship and Accountability</u>
Who is responsible and accountable for the production, use and distribution of the resources of the earth? How should the irresponsibility and wastefulness of God's resources be handled?

6. <u>Global Geography</u>
The quality of life is determined to a significant degree by where a person is born or live on the earth. How can the standard and quality of life be more balanced on a global scale?

7. <u>Human Heterogeneity</u>
There is a wide variety of differences among human beings. These differences are often exploited. They often cause division, discrimination and disharmony. How can human differences be used creatively and innovatively to enhance and enrich human life instead of degrading and dividing?

8. <u>Racial Genetics and Ethnic Sectarianism</u>
Racial, ethnic and sectarian differences are root causes of great pain losses and even death. How can racial and ethnic prejudices be overcome and parity as human beings be reached? How can there be complements, blending and balance among r a c i a l and ethnic groups?

9. <u>Ethical Relativity and Moral Neutrality</u>
Increased personal freedom allows individuals and groups to be more autonomous in their choices and life styles. Therefore, there is growing confusion in regards to ethical and moral values. How can a universal moral/ethical standard be established based on sound doctrine and validated truth?

10. <u>National Patriotism vs. Globalism</u>
There is a growing trend for individuals to go to other countries to live and obtain citizenship. However, a significant number of these immigrating individuals choose to remain loyal to their original country, religions and customs. Therefore, diverse nations, religions, alien customs and cultures are being established in the host countries. Some of the religions, customs and cultures conflict with those of the host country. How long can the host country safely, accommodate growing nations within its nation and remain a unified nation? How can national patriotism be harmonized with global patriotism?

11. <u>Autonomous Technology</u>
Technology is wreaking monumental changes on society, its people, institutions and culture. These changes are taking place with such rapidity that there is not sufficient time to adjust to one change before the institution of the next change. There are three major downsides to these changes.

(1) Many people are being left behind and left out because they do not possess the technological resources or skills to keep pace with the rapid changes. Many rights and entitlements guaranteed by the U. S. Constitution are being forfeited because of the inability of a substantial number of citizens

to participate. Gross violations of civil rights are taking place because of technology and no one seems interested in addressing these violations.

(2) The traditional and manual ways of doing things are being discarded. Even the bridges, the means and methods of getting things done the traditional way are being torn down and burned down. Society is racing toward total dependence on technology. There are serious flaws and fallacies involved in the total dependence on technology. The most significant fallacy is the failure to fully recognize the fact that technology requires electric power. Electric power can cut off or go out. This is an example of autonomous technology. It is devoid of human national guidance. It has a morbid momentum of its own.

(3) The third downside is there is no credible or competent agency, institution, committee or commission to study, monitor, guide, plan and recommend on the effects of technological changes on short range and long range quality of human life, human society and human culture. What is the impact of technology on moral and ethical values? How can technology be harmonized in conformance to the Will of God and uplifting humanity? How can technology be responsibly guided?

12. <u>Environmental Stewardship</u>
Who is responsible and who is assigned to the protection and the maintenance of the environment of the earth? Where are the global, universal laws to protect and maintain the environment of the earth? Who is responsible for the enforcement of these laws? Why is not the sacred planetary habitat of life on earth universally respected and revered as a gift of God?

Summary

It is most unfortunate, and even tragic that Christian public theology is not accepted as a major role player in the public decision-making in the American society. However, it must be acknowledged that the American Civil Rights Movement spearheaded by Dr. Martin Luther King, Jr. along with other ministers in the 1960s was a public theological movement. Dr. King was a Baptist minister and pastor of Dexter Avenue Baptist Church in Montgomery, Alabama. When he was called to be the president of the Southern Christian Leadership Conference and the Montgomery Bus Boycott leader. It must also be noted that the theological leaders in the Civil Rights Movement were exceptional because the mainstream black and white ministers were not in favor of the minister-led Civil Rights Movement. Many of the ministers in the North and South, black and white were critical of Dr. King and the movement. History has vindicated Dr. King and validated the value and role of public theology.

The statutory laws throughout the southern part of the United States not only condoned the separation of the races but there were laws that required the separation of races in public accommodations during the 1960 civil rights era. Although the atrocities of racial segregation and discrimination were more rampant in the South, the U. S. federal government did nothing to correct the discriminatory laws and protect the rights of black United States citizens. We cannot just blame the South for the atrocities, because the highest lawmakers of the U. S. government were complicit in the violations.

It was the theological-led Civil Rights Movement that persuaded the U. S. courts to pass civil rights legislation to correct the unjust discriminatory laws. This is just one of many examples where the theological perspective was needed to correct manmade statutory laws. It was the theological perspective of nonviolent protest, under girded by love, righteousness and justice that brought about changes in America more in line with the Will of God.

Public theology is advocating theological consultation instead of theological confrontation. It would have been much less costly and much less tragic during the Civil Rights Movement to peacefully consult and confer rather than to confront with the violence of police dogs, clubs, water hoses, tear gas, and arrests. Looking back in retrospect, it is incumbent upon us to employ the insightful education that we learned by engaging public theology in the public domains of decision making. More public theologians must be employed in government, business and the corporate world at large. Public theologians can make great contributions to agencies, businesses, government, corporations and other institutions as they work, direct and sit on various boards. Christianity and democracy are highly compatible. They must form a closer union and working relationship to maintain freedom and human rights. Public theology must imitate this union with all agencies and institutions in the society.

    Public theology bridges the gap between the lost and found, ignorance and knowledge, rich and poor, the human and the divine, the secular and sacred, the spiritual and the material, falsehood and truth, the kingdom of the world and the kingdom of God.

Chapter 5

The Problem for Public Theology

1. Theological consultation is absent in the making of crucial policies, laws, decisions and plans from the local to the national and international levels that have significant impact on the lives of all people and the total environment. The elimination and discouragement of theology in public decision-making is an ongoing tragedy. How can public theology assure that the word, ways, wisdom and Will of God be incorporated in the decision making process where the public welfare is concerned?

2. The misunderstanding of the separation of church and state doctrine and the misinterpretation of the First Amendment rights have led to legal decisions that promote a public life that is free of religion in general and Christianity in particular. What is the proper relationship between church and state?

3. The separation of church and state doctrine has escalated significantly, the secularization of public education from preschool, elementary school through

high school, colleges and universities. Can society afford this significant theological education deficit in the public educational system?

4. Contemporary political culture emphasizes individual liberty and a broad array of individual rights often at the expense of the commitment to the common good of all. This mode of "selfish expressive individualism" prevents many people from committing to anything beyond their own selfish interests. What happens to the community when everyone begins to stray away into individual selfish indulgence?

5. The growing abdication of moral responsibility to society and the growing fragmentation of society have made it difficult for authoritative voices to be heard and respected. How can individual moral obligation to society and the common good be achieved with this emphasis on individualism and its subsequent fragmentation?

6. American life is floundering in a sea of cultural, political, moral, religious and ethical pluralism and relativism without a recognized common vision and clear direction for all. How can a common vision and true direction for the common good in this sea of diversity be established?

7. Civil liberties unions and their allies are working to eliminate religious/Christian expressions in the public sectors. Is statutory legal authority sufficiently authorized by the U. S. Constitution and the divine law of God to limit or restrict religious/Christian expressions in the public sector?

8. American democracy provides freedom and protection of religion. The religious caption includes

a variety of cults and sectarian groups. Some of these religious and sectarian groups have proved to be harmful to their members as well as society. What is a valid religion? How can society be safeguarded from false religions?

9. There appears to be a growing state of ethical and moral confusion. Biblical authority and truth have become (in the minds of many people) relative and irrelevant. Therefore, many decisions are not made on the basis of sound doctrine and truth. Critical decisions regarding the rights, safety, liberty and the life of others are often arbitrary decisions. Arbitrary decisions are random and whimsical. They violate the rules of logic, truth, righteousness and justice. How can respect and adherence to sound doctrine, truth, moral and ethical values be restored?

10. The creeds of America, which acknowledge a belief in God, seem to have served America well. The creeds of America embody the Declaration of Independence, U. S. Constitution, Emancipation Proclamation, and Pledge of Allegiance along with the U. S. motto, which is inscribed on its currency, "In God We Trust." The history of America confirms its founding and establishment upon the Christian principles of the Holy Bible. These principles are woven into the fabric of American life. Can anything good or valuable come out of the current trend to de-Christianize America?

11. America has a democracy and a tradition of embracing immigrants with their different languages, cultures, nationalities, races and religions. Well over 40 million immigrants have come to America within the past 50 years. Many of the immigrants resist the assimilation into the American culture. Many are

asserting their own cultures and the way of life they practiced before coming to America. Some are in America to change the American way of life. There are also immigrants and non-immigrant Americans who are anti America and anti Christian who harbor sentiments to destroy America. There is no effective screening to determine who these individuals are. Increasingly, Americans are becoming enmeshed and interdependent with strangers and strange doctrines. How can individuals in a diverse and pluralistic society who depend on vital services and goods from strangers be protected in vulnerable services and goods, such as healthcare services, pharmaceutical products, food supplies and food preparation, water supply, transportation, communication, construction industry, etc.?

12. There are some human engineered acts of violence in the world that are clearly against humanity and civilization itself. There are human engineered acts of violence in the world to defend humanity and civilization. Some people are systematically taught from their youth to hate and kill other human beings in the name of God. What is the distinction between killing to destroy humanity and killing to save humanity? Is it morally and ethically responsible to be neutral when children (especially) are being taught to hate and kill in the name of God?

Summary and Conclusion

The enumerated problems and questions above are not necessarily new questions or new problems. People have always hated and perpetrated violence and death against each other. What is new is the ability and the capacity to harm and kill more people in more ways because of the advances in scientific technology. The availability of technology to multiply the expression of hatred and evil is the new quantity in the equation of warfare. The great challenge facing humanity in the 21st century is to avoid human destruction through the misguided use of technology. The flip side of this challenge is to use technology in strategic and positive ways to help and to save humanity. The answers and the solutions to the problems, questions and challenges are available in the contextual engagement of theology. The answers are biblically based in the word of God as they are theologically guided by the mind of Christ.

CHAPTER 6

Critical Questions for the Public Theologian

There may not be a ready-made answer for the following questions below. However, if the appropriate and relevant questions can be formulated and asked, the search for the answers can begin. New situations and new circumstances require new reflections, new perspectives and new contextual responses. Raising the right questions makes it possible to employ reason, investigation and analysis in search for the answers. When the questions are raised, the process of finding the answers has begun. Delays and procrastinations in crisis situations can be costly and irreversible. While there is still time (although it is late) let the process of theological inquiry and intervention begin with the following critical questions:

1. How can Christians most effectively manifest (practice) the spirit of Jesus Christ and his ministry of service, love, hope, faith, freedom, brother/sisterhood, healing, liberation, transformation and leadership in a public domain that is growing more and more hostile to Christianity?

2. How must the Christians and the Church defend themselves and society from the increasing

proliferation of false doctrines, false religions and the escalating antichrists?

3. What resources do Christians have and what strategies and methodologies must Christians employ to counteract the aggression of the false religions, the escalating antichrist spirits and the passivity of many persons who identify themselves as Christians?

4. How must American Democracy provide limitations and safeguards within its broad policies of inclusive accommodations, toleration and immigration to diverse cultures, political, religious and belief systems of people throughout the earth and simultaneously, protect the democracy, human freedom and the foundation values rooted in Christianity?

5. How can the Christian Church move from rhetorical emotionalism, political impotence and public indifference to confronting the culture crisis through social empowerment and public involvement?

6. How must the public theologian provide a universally valid foundation for Christians (along with allied believers) to live, love and serve the children of God wherever they may be, in the private or public domain?

7. How can America, intelligently and wisely, affirm pluralism and diversity without diluting and corroding the core values of America and rending the fragile garment that holds together the common good for all?

8. How must the public theologians and the Church relate to, give guidance, invitation and transformation, to the increasing cultural diversity, internationalism,

and religious pluralism in America, to avoid the inevitable destructive separation, isolation and societal fragmentation?

9. Can Christianity in America be relegated to the same status and level of other religions in America without disavowing Jesus as the only begotten Son of God and without invalidating the validity of Christianity?

10. What inspirations, persuasions and motivations can be used to convince the pastors, ministers, churches and religious leaders, (in the face of lethal challenges to the church and the world) to invest significantly, more money, time and resources to prepare the clergy and the laity for effective spiritual warfare?

11. What strategies and recommendations can you offer as a public theologian to build more solid security systems in the following areas: spiritual security, social security, economic security, educational security, political security, cultural security, religious security, environmental security, personal security?

12. What source of legitimate authority and what vital qualifications are needed to lead a culturally diverse, heterogeneous and pluralistic society for humanity in the global community?

Summary and Conclusions

These questions are placed on the doorsteps of the church and in the lap of the theologians. The church and theology cannot continue to hold on to their credibility and spiritual dignity if they evade these questions and fail to address them. When the questions and problems of society get too complex and difficult for the social, political and natural sciences, theology must get involved in providing the ultimate answers.

Chapter 7

The Invitation of Public Theology

The invitation of public theology is an invitation to practice the tenets of religion in public life. Christian theology proclaims the most ethical and enlightened standards known to humankind. These standards are contained in the Holy Bible for all people. These enlightened standards of living have not been sufficiently taught or practiced in the public domain. It is the responsibility of the Christian theologians to get the knowledge of life in the heads, the hearts, the practice and the institutions of people in public life. The deprivation of the Gospel of Christ and the privatization of the Judeo-Christian religion are not sufficient substitutes for the public expression of the Gospel and the public acknowledgement of God.

Therefore, the invitation of public theology makes the following recommendations:

1. Move away from the "Mars Hill Syndrome," of continuous debates, discussions and discourses, and move to meeting the practical long list of needs that exist all around us in our communities. The victims and the victimizers are rampant in the society. Rhetorical discourses are not sufficient to meet these needs.

2. Move away from the theories of love, religion and philosophy to the practice of the fatherhood of God and the brotherhood and the sisterhood of humanity. The practice of love is more important than the expounding of theories.

3. There are many lofty private creeds that need to be transitioned into the public arena of deeds. The challenge is to get beyond the indulgence of talk to the demonstration of the work and the walk.

4. How can lip service be translated into knowledge of the head, skills of the hand, compassion of the heart and service to those in need? There is a temptation and a tendency to talk too much and too long and to do too little too late. More must be done.

5. Public theology is an invitation to overcome passivity, indifference and neutrality and get decisively involved in community and public affairs. There is no safe recluse-hiding place for anyone. The danger is at the door. It must be met before it breaks in.

6. There must be movement from non-commitment to commissioned discipleship. The culture crisis requires that theology move from sideline observation to frontline participation with passion, purpose and a God guided plan.

7. The Church is challenged to move from the retreat of private consumption to the position of public production. The Church must not concede cowardice and defeat. It must initiate bold witness and courage for victory and triumph. It must inspire human dignity and master builders and authoritative leaders.

8. Public theology offers leadership that moves away from a culture engulfed in sensate pleasure and childhood irresponsibility to the duty and responsibility of mature adulthood. Divisions and fragmentations must give way to unity, togetherness and peace.

9. Move away from the destructive influences of the idol gods to the living, life giving omnipotent eternal God in Jesus Christ. Righteousness, goodness, truth and light have been demonstrated in history with infallible proofs. The way to life has been made clear for all people.

10. Public theology is a movement away from private exclusive selfish self-centeredness to a focus on community, public concerns and what is in the best interest of the common good of all. There is one world, one God and one humanity.

11. Public theology must invite the people of God away from blind leadership, unauthorized hierarchies and dysfunctional bureaucracies to follow prophetic visions, spiritual guidance, and the wisdom of God, the light of the world and the mind of Jesus Christ.

12. Public theology is an invitation to the people of God to rise above being dominated and oppressed, to those peculiar people who transform cultures, enrich humanity, provide guardianship of truth, shine light in darkness, provide leadership in diversity, elevate civilization, be fruitful and multiply and exercise dominion over the earth as accountable stewards of God.

The Holy Bible is humanity's blueprint and master plan for living and survival. It is a plan that comes from God. It has the authoritative answers for man's life and destiny. The Bible has set the standards for human relationships. It has set the standards for man's relationship to God. God has set the standards for his people and given commandments on how all people must live their lives. It is tragic that most people in the world and most people in America do not know sufficiently the message of God. It is urgent that the theologians begin in a bold intentional manner to make known the word of God in the public square.

CHAPTER 8

Guiding Themes for Public Theology

The guiding themes set forth in this chapter are not meant to be exhaustive. They are not meant to be complex or confusing. The aim is to enumerate simple and practical themes that are relevant and understandable for the average and reasonable intelligence. These guiding themes encompass the objectives, goals and challenges for public theology. They also outline the work and the mission for CAPT (Christian Association of Public Theologians) and CIPT (Christian Institute of Public Theology).

Guiding Themes

1. A Christian theology that spiritually undergirds and transforms the social interactions, function, and directions of society, construct vehicles to convey the sound Christian theological doctrine throughout the society by way of teaching, preaching, practice and service into the public domain. This guiding theme is geared towards transforming the culture into more civil, humane, ethical and moral values.

2. Establish a public theology for guiding the humanitarian use of science. To provide the most advanced Christian theological guidance and humanitarian purpose for the peaceful use of scientific technology and scientific technology intelligence. Ultimately, public theology must provide the guidance and the rationale for the development and use of scientific technology in a globalized world. The intricate ethical, moral, cultural and religious complexities are so vast that a science with a vertical theological dimension must be used to fathom the answers.

3. It is mandatory that public theology assists the government and the bureaucratic operations of society to be aware of the existing moral, ethical and humanitarian standards for the operation of government over the human affairs of society. This can be accomplished, in part, by providing the Christian theological framework for the development of policies, principles and ethical codes for the institutional administration of justice, commerce, industry, righteousness, peace and liberty. Because Christian theology is compatible with democratic philosophy, there is no conflict of interest between Church and state. A predominant Christian population in the United States for the past 230 years have never advocated and have never sought a Christian theocracy in America. This overwhelming Christian population in America has tolerated and accommodated people of diverse cultures, nationalities, religions, races and ethnicities. It must also be noted that the Christian principles and the Christian posture in America would not tolerate or accommodate any religious sectarian ruled government in America.

4. The advent of globalization has made it necessary and even urgent for public theology to play a significant role in defining the hierarchy of legitimate authority. Public theology has the responsibility in establishing universally, true values and sound principles for global community living based on the noblest principles and the highest benevolent authority known to humankind. What person, group of persons, ideas, concepts, principles, or creeds that have been ordained by God to be the final and ultimate authority to exercise dominion over God's people? It is the duty of public theology to arrive at a legitimate rational answer to this question. It must not be arbitrary.

5. Public theology must establish standards of Christian ethics that determines what is right, true and just in all human interactions and human relations. A theological basis must be established along with the scientific method and inquiry that can be used objectively and rationally to reflect, calculate, evaluate and validate factual reality, true principles and valid principles in the areas of science, law, ethics, art and religion, to avoid arbitrary decisions, unsound doctrines and subsequent injurious actions. A globalized world with potent technological specimen, instruments and armaments, makes it critically important to narrow the margins of error. It is critically important to be accurate in intellectual deliberations and precise in decision-making. Mistakes in judgments can be lethal, costly and catastrophic.

6. There is a major and dangerous theological knowledge void in most every society. Public theology must work to overcome this void and theological knowledge deficit by supporting and advocating major investments (time, money, energy, skills, resources) in holistic education and Christian ethical

training. It must provide a Christian theological rationale and concerted leadership to eradicate human ignorance, injustice and evil through sound contextual education, training, ethics, treatment and skills for Christian living. Too many individuals are making erroneous theological decisions because they do not have theological training or adequate theological knowledge.

7. The restrictions of religious education and involvement in the public school systems as well as other government agencies, has limited the opportunity for the transmission of moral, ethical and spiritual values. Character development in the youth of society is left to chance. It is the role of public theology to make a concerted effort to ensure that ethical, moral spiritual and character development training is a part of the public education curriculum. Public theology must bridge the gaps among the home, school, church and community to allow for the transmission of ethical values and the optimum opportunity for character development.

8. It is the role of public theology to go beyond the boundaries and the barriers that separate human beings and make the theological connection. The public theologian must be sensitive and considerate, but also bold in assisting individuals and groups to rise above and transcend narrow loyalties, conflicting interests, blind passions, and selfish ambitions in order to serve and provide inclusive leadership for the common good of all humanity and God loving people. The public theologian must be bold in providing the true historical theological rationale for proclaiming and witnessing the universal and all human inclusiveness of Jesus Christ as the only begotten son of God and savior of the world. This

proclamation is not exclusive to any individual. God is all-inclusive.

9. Moral and religious relativism, ethical neutrality, and individual self-centered ethnocentrism are generating confusion and moral decay. In the midst of this confusion and decay, the public theologian must point the way of righteousness, justice, peace and salvation for all humanity based on the highest authority in the revealed word of God. The public theologian must proclaim liberation and salvation theology that has been validated in history for over two thousand years and witnessed by over two billion people on the earth. The challenge is to get the practice of this Gospel beyond the church walls into the mainstream and the public market place. It must be done with bold clarity.

10. Public theology must formulate, embrace, practice and teach moral codes of ethics. The belief in truth; the practice of ethical conduct; the cultivation of spiritual values and a commitment to love and forgive must become inherent in the institutions and the culture of society. The consistent wide spread practice of moral codes, ethical conduct, guided by the most advanced spiritual creeds, can transform individuals, groups, institutions, cultures and society. Vast numbers of people are going astray because they have no credible guides. Public theology must point the way clearly for all humanity.

11. Individuals, organizations, churches, other institutions and societies can become stuck and complacent in the status quo of indifference and lostness. Public theology, with its prophetic voice, spiritual insight and vision, must be able to see what is and proclaim what ought to be. It must also point the way, chart

the course and establish conditions on how to get where God wants his people to be and do things of God's Will.

12. Disparities of injustice and inequities are rampant in most societies. Such conditions contribute to poverty, crime, pain, suffering and death. A public theology working in conjunction with the church is needed to provide redemptive services to the poor and disadvantaged, for liberation, healing, nurture, restoration, spiritual growth, mature stewardship and responsibility for human health and wholeness. Public theology is challenged to train and certify skilled human helpers within the church, as well as centers of help and hope established in the communities for deliverance and empowerment.

CHAPTER 9

Foundations for Biblical Understanding

It is essential that some basic elements regarding the Bible be understood in order to be an effective and credible practitioner of public theology. The same basic elements of understanding the Bible are also required for a theological Christian education. A theological Christian education is meant to refer to a rational approach to the study of the Bible with respect to factual knowledge and validated sound doctrine as opposed to subjective opinionated emotionalism and relativism. Since the focus of this book is practical theology, it is important to maintain a rational approach with intellectual respectability. The aim is for clarity, enlightenment and to enhance the understanding and the comprehensive use of the Bible in the practice of public theology.

The following elements or prerequisites for understanding the Bible are given without extensive elaboration or exhaustive explanation. It is a brief survey of things to consider to broaden our understanding of the Bible to provide a fund of knowledge and foundation for the broad practice of public theology:

1. The Bible as an Historical Document
   The Holy Bible must be appreciated and understood as a unique historical document. It is a historical documented account of the people of Israel and their covenant relationship with God. It is not a book of mythology. It is not a book of mystical perceptions. It is a book that gives an account of a specified people, over a specified period of time. It provides the names of designated places on the earth and the records of events in the context of historical circumstances. The Bible provides the names of its characters and the genealogy from Adam to Jesus Christ. The Old Testament is about God's creation and God's covenants and promises to Israel. The New Testament is about the coming, birth, life, teachings, disciples, crucifixion, resurrection, commission and ascension of Jesus Christ. The words of Jesus and the acts of Jesus are so significant that, both, his words and acts became good news for all time. The coming of Jesus is recorded as the most significant event of history. He is the only individual that stands in the center of history. Time is counted backwards as B. C. (Before Christ) and it is counted forward from his coming as A. D. (Anno Domini) in the year of our Lord. The Christian calendar with Jesus at the center of history cannot be honestly or rationally denied. Any denial of the historicity of Jesus becomes void when it is dated. Because the date itself acknowledges the Jesus of history. Jesus is at the center of the Old Testament and the New Testament.

2. Historical Progressive Revelation
   Study the Bible as God's progressive revelation in history. The Bible is a historical record of God's dynamic spiritual interaction between God's revelation to mankind and mankind's response to that revelation. The Bible records the beginning

of these revelations and interactions. The ideas, concepts, doctrines and covenants can be traced from Genesis through Revelation. The Bible is the most unique development of history. It is the greatest story ever told. It contains the record of God's disclosure of himself and truth; and man's search, discovery and response to God's disclosure. The development of the Bible grew from crude beginnings until it reached its zenith in Jesus Christ exemplifying the most advanced and the most refined human values known to humankind.

3. <u>The Universal Scope of the Bible</u>
It is essential to understand the universal scope and application of the Holy Bible. The message of the Bible speaks to all humanity for all time. The Bible establishes God as the creator of everything with the sole jurisdiction over all creation.

4. <u>The Bible's Continuing Relevance</u>
The Bible contains the highest ethical standards for moral conduct, positive attitudes, religious aspirations, personal actualizations, social and spiritual salvation for all humanity. It must be understood that humanity never outgrows or advances beyond the need for the revelatory message of the Bible. There is no other comparable volume known to history to be as historical, accurate, complete, congruent and true as the Holy Bible. No creature can legitimately claim to be neutral or indifferent to the Bible. Individuals and groups may be disobedient to its laws and rebellious to its commandments. However, no one can indefinitely escape the consequences of its judgment.

5. <u>Biblical Sound Doctrine</u>
The sound doctrine of the Bible has endured for over two thousand years. It has lived through all of the ideologies and philosophies known to humankind. It has withstood the test of time as the enduring wisdom of the ages. The Bible has survived all manner of false doctrines. It has already survived materialism, racism, nationalism, cultism, sectarianism, atheism, paganism, heathenism, humanism, skepticism, stoicism, epicureanism, mysticism, scholasticism and all manner of heresies and idolatries. There is every evidence that the writers of the Bible, wrote as they were inspired by God. The writers expanded over four thousand years. They could not have known what subsequent writers would say. However, there is a master Spirit behind the writings that make them connected, congruent and authoritative. All the writers have long been silenced in death, but their message continues to speak with sound doctrine and abiding truth. The Bible is a book of validated truth and sound doctrine.

6. <u>The Contextual Use of Scripture</u>
The interpretation of Scripture must take into consideration the time period, the place, the circumstances and purpose of the particular event or circumstance in order to understand the truth of the respective scripture. Although the Scripture may be interpreted and transposed for the present time, it is essential to consider the context of scriptural origination. All scripture must be understood and interpreted in the light of Jesus Christ for appropriate present application. The mind of Christ is the key to the correct interpretation of Scripture. "It has been said of them of old time ... but I say unto you."

7. <u>Distinguishing Exegesis and Eisegesis</u>
One who attempts to teach, preach, interpret or practice what the Scripture says must be able to distinguish between the meaning of exegesis and eisegesis. Exegesis means interpreting the scripture based on what the respective scripture actually states. Eisegesis means reading into the Scripture a personal interpretation that the actual written Scripture did not state. Eisegesis means to read into the Scripture one's own opinion or one's personal interpretation devoid of the literal statement of Scripture. Be clear on exegeting and eisegeting.

8. <u>The Bible and Human Nature</u>
The Bible records God's creation of man and woman, male and female. Since God created human nature, among other things, the Bible is a reflection of the complex manifestations of human nature in all of its varied forms. Increased understanding of the Bible brings about an increased understanding of human nature. The truth of the Bible is intimately acquainted with man and knows man through and through. The Bible is an exegesis on human nature. The Bible knows man's human potential for descending into the depths of hell or into the lofty heights of heaven. One of the reasons that the Bible maintains its relevance for humanity after thousands of years is because it is interwoven with human nature. As long as there is human nature the message of the Bible will be relevant to understand, heal nurture and redeem that human nature through love, mercy, forgiveness, hope, salvation and grace.

9. <u>Human Nature and Human Nurture</u>
Human nature or the potential for the development of human nature is passed on from parents to their off spring through a genetic, biological and physiological

process. To that extent a child is born into the world with the rudiments of human nature. The culture and the interaction of the social environment add to this human nature of the growing and developing human organism another dimension known as human nurture. Human nurture is the influence and effects that the social environment and culture have on the growing and developing human individual. Human nature and human nurture can result in high degrees of human socialization, cultivation and acculturation. Significant accomplishments can be obtained through humanism. In spite of the potential for humanism to advance, theologically speaking, it is still on the horizontal human level. In order to be freed or transcend humanistic nature and nurture, a vertical dimension must be added. The vertical dimension suggests a new nature that comes from God. Jesus made reference to this new nature when he told Nicodemus, "You must be born again." Great credit must be given to what can and has been accomplished on the horizontal humanistic plane through biology, physiology, chemistry, sociology, psychology, political science and other artistic and scientific disciplines. Theology adds the vertical dimension for acquiring the new nature and becoming a new creature in Christ. At their best, human nature and human nurture are not sufficient for spiritual wholeness and salvation. The good news of theology is that God offers a new nature that transcends and supersedes the old nature. This new nature is above culture and has the power to transform culture. This new nature and new creature-hood is found in Jesus Christ.

10. <u>The Bible as a Holistic Entity</u>
It is essential for all persons who wish to understand the Bible and teach others that the Bible is analogous to a living organismic entity. That is to say that the

Bible had a beginning or birth in history. After its birth, it grew and developed as a child grows and develops from childhood, adolescence, and young adulthood to full adulthood. The ideas and concepts of the contents of the Bible grew and changed over the centuries. When inconsistencies are observed in the Bible, it is important to assess the particular stage of development of the Bible at that time in history. The developing stages grew, matured and culminated in the coming of Jesus Christ. Jesus Christ represents the full adulthood of the living word of the Bible. Just as we do not judge adults by their childhood and youthful behavior, we do not judge the Bible by certain inconsistencies and crudities in its developmental stages. We judge the Bible by what it came to be in its fulfillment in Jesus Christ. Jesus Christ is the truth and the standard of truth. He is the High Priest and highest authority. He came not to destroy the laws or the prophets, but to fulfill them. Jesus acknowledges the Old Testament writings without criticism. However, one of his primary themes in the fifth chapter of Matthew was, "It has been said of them of old time ... but I say unto you."

11. The Universality of Jesus Christ

The language that is used to describe Jesus in the Bible is universal language. God so loved the world that he gave his only begotten Son. He is the light of the world. In the beginning was the word and the word was with God and the word was God. The word became flesh and dwelt among us. There is no other name under heaven given among men whereby we must be saved. Every knee shall bow and every tongue confess that Jesus is Lord. He came not to condemn the world, but to save the world. He is Lord of lords, and King of kings. His commission to his disciples was to go into all the world and teach all nations. He is living water and the bread of life. He is the door. That door is a universal door that is open to all people who are willing to believe and receive Jesus. Jesus came not to condemn the world. He came not to destroy the laws or the prophets. He came not to negate any truth, or goodness or beauty in any religion of philosophy. He is the fulfillment of all truth, goodness, righteousness and beauty. Jesus Christ is a unique revelation of God in history. Jesus is the most composite and most complete revelation of God. On one occasion, Jesus told his listeners that no man has seen God at any time. He said further, "If you have seen me, you have seen the Father." The uniqueness of Jesus has not been duplicated in history. It must be noted that antichrist spirits are working hard to deny the revelation of God in Jesus in history. Some of these antichrist spirits have begun to substitute B. C. (Before Christ) for BCE (Before Common Era) and they are substituting A. D. (Anno Domini – In the year of our Lord) for ACE (After Common Era). These substitutions are bold and gross misrepresentations of the established truth of history. The BCE and the ACE are the stealthy encroachments of lies into literature that must be refuted on the grounds of dishonesty and a malevolent disregard for ethics and truth. Jesus is the reason for the dates that are used from day to day. The Christian calendar and the computerized dates testify that Jesus is at the center of history. Jesus alone, marks that point in history where humanity began to count backwards to what has been and forward to the future. Today's date is the concrete global evidence that Jesus is the only individual at the center of history.

12. The Old and New Testament Connection

The Old Testament describes the beginning of creation, the creation of mankind and the birth and development of the Hebrew religion, beginning with Abraham, Isaac and Jacob. The 39 books of the Old Testament consist of five books of law, 12 books of history, four books of wisdom and 17 books of prophets. These books consist of God's revelations, promises and covenant relationship with the people of Israel. The Hebrew religion, known as Judaism, contained a number of sectarian groups. Christianity was born in Judaism. It started as one of the sectarian groups of Judaism. The Pharisees, Sadducees, Essenes and Zealots were sectarian groups. Jesus was a Jew born of the lineage of David. The birth, person, teaching, crucifixion, resurrection and ascension of Jesus gave rise to Christianity. In the Old Testament, God promised to establish an eternal kingdom in the house of King David. Approximately one thousand years later, Jesus was born in Bethlehem according to biblical prophecy. Jesus became the fulfillment of the promises of the Old Testament. Revelations says, "He is the root and the offspring of David." There are an overwhelming number of confirmations in the New Testament that Jesus is the promise and fulfillment of the Old Testament. The Old Testament and the New Testament have been closed with 66 books. It is a complete book for all humanity. The Christians embrace the complete book. Therefore, the Christians are prepared to embrace all humanity – the world.

__Summary__

Foundations for biblical understanding are provided to enhance the broad understanding of the Bible, especially for the public theologian. It contains the foundation principles, the mission and the authority for the practice of public theology. The Bible is inclusive and universal. It contains the greatest story ever told. It is the story of the human race in its relationship to God for all time.

Chapter 10

The Christian Role in Diversity

God and Religion

God and religion are not synonymous. God with the capital "G" is not relegated to religion, science, art, government, law or any other discipline or phenomenon known to mankind. God is not just sovereign over earthly affairs. God is the creator and sustainer of all creation.

It is ludicrous to attempt to restrict or limit God to any religion, belief system, ritual or any place of worship. It is also absurd to attempt to restrict or limit God to earth, the solar system or even the universe itself; not to mention religion, society, government and cultural systems on the earth. It is preposterous for finite beings to conclude that there is no infinite God. The absolute power and magnitude of God is beyond the logic and comprehension of human beings.

Validated theological knowledge confirms that God is eternal (no beginning or ending), infinite (boundless), omnipotent (all powerful), omniscient (all knowing), omnipresent (present everywhere), immortal (not subject to death), absolute (complete self sufficient wholeness). This theological knowledge about God and the nature of God is disclosed by God's creation. Take a look at the sky, the stars, and the vastness of space. God is revealed through the special revelation of the Holy Scripture as recorded in the Holy Bible. There is no other literary volume known to history with over two thousand years of spiritual continuity from Genesis to Revelation.

The distinction must be made between the Creator God and the idol gods. There are many idol gods that are spelled with a small "g." Mankind is capable of bowing down and worshipping all manner of gods. Man has a history of worshipping animate and inanimate things. These objects of worship, known as idol gods range from trees, rocks, the moon, the sun, animals and other human beings. Man can also worship religious objects, religious symbols and religion itself. Anything that man worships other than God is idol worship or idolatry.

It is a gross mistake to equate God and religion as being synonymous. Religions consist of beliefs, value systems, rituals, ceremonies and objects of adoration and worship. It is evident that true religions are inspired by God. Nevertheless religious belief systems are created and built by man as a means toward an end. A religion cannot be an end within itself and be valid. Because religions are created by man for various and sundry reasons, religions are subject to be valid and invalid, true or false.

Religions are created or born within cultures and societies. Religions can be spawn by other religions, various types of organizations and charismatic leaders. Many religions develop, grow and flourish.

Many religions are born and die at various stages of development. As far as can be determined at this time in history, religion is a phenomenon of the earth practiced by mortal human beings.

This brief synopsis of religion is provided to highlight the vast differences between the characteristics of religion and the characteristics of God. It can be readily seen from the contrast between the concept of religion and the concept of God that God and religion are not synonymous. However, this gross mistake of using God and religion as being synonymous happens routinely in the American society and in the American press. Unfortunately, it is not just lay people, but professional and educated people equate God and religion as being synonymous. And worst of all, many executive, legislative and judicial decisions are made with the erroneous notion that God and religion are synonymous.

The acknowledgement of God is not the same as worshipping or advocating the worship of God. It is more natural and logical to acknowledge the existence of God than it is to deny or be oblivious to the existence of God. The word of God as used on U. S. currency, the Declaration of Independence and the Pledge of Allegiance are examples of the acknowledgement of God and not the religious worship or advocacy for religious worship of God. The acknowledgement and reference to God can be and is often used in a non-religious sense.

If an argument is needed for the existence of God, there exists clear, convincing and overwhelming evidence in the cosmological nature of the universe. Human existence and human consciousness offer evidence for the existence of God. It is obvious to any reasonable intelligence that there is a power much higher than humankind. There is visible and discernible evidence that declares there is God.

On the contrary there is no credible evidence to suggest that there is no God. Therefore, it must be concluded that it is unnatural, invalid and arbitrary for any statutory law or manmade decision to prohibit human beings from acknowledging God privately or publicly.

Christ and Christianity

Jesus Christ and Christianity are not synonymous. Salvation is not found or promised in the religion of Christianity. It is not found in the church building, in the pulpit, in the pool or the communion or any designated place or service. It is not found in the ceremonies and rituals, the singing or the preaching. Salvation is found in the person of Jesus Christ.

The religion of Christianity was founded by Jesus Christ and established upon the rock of faith in Christ. Christianity and the followers of Christ, called Christians, have done and accomplished marvelous and incredible good works in history. Over two billion people on the planet earth identify themselves as Christians. The spiritual salvation of the believer is not found in the religion. It is found in Christ.

Christianity is an organized effort and institutionalized structure to carry out the Great Commission of Jesus Christ. The great universal commission of Jesus Christ is an outreach of forgiveness and an invitation of embrace by the love of God. The God in Jesus Christ does not force his Will. God reveals his Will and allows the individual to choose to obey or disobey. Christianity is a redemptive means for learning about the works, ways, wisdom, and the practice of God's Will through preaching, teaching and service. In spite of all the good works of Christianity, the religion, itself is not synonymous with Jesus Christ.

Shedding Light of Misconceptions

1. Becoming a Christian is a Personal Choice
   There are persons who make the assumption that Christianity is imposed on others. This is a false assumption. It must be emphatically stated that it is against the tenets of Christianity to force anyone to be a Christian or to force Christian views on others. Christians are led to be believers in Christ through their own free will motivated by love and the desire for salvation. An individual becomes a Christian, not by outside force or intimidation, but by inside conviction.

   One does not become a Christian through genetics, family, racial or national inheritance. A person becomes a Christian through personal choice. It is significant to note that God creates human beings to be free. God gives freedom of thought to human beings. God gives the freedom to choose to human beings. God gives choices for human decisions. This freedom that God gives is intrinsic in Jesus Christ. God through Jesus Christ respects the autonomous integrity of human beings. God gives the human being the autonomy and freedom to serve God or idols. Any religion or system of thought that forces or attempts to force a person to believe against his conscious or to take away the freedom of thought is a violation of a God given unalienable right of individual autonomy. God has not given any person or agency the right to rob another human being of his soul. Serious committed acceptance of Jesus Christ means that the believer becomes a disciple or follower of Jesus Christ. Jesus is accepted as Savior to bring redemption, transformation, liberation and eternal salvation. He is accepted as Lord to rule the believer's life.

2. <u>Salvation Cannot Be Earned</u>

The Bible teaches that man cannot earn salvation through his actions of his righteousness. Salvation is a gift of God through faith and belief in Jesus Christ. This gift of salvation is given exclusively by God through Jesus Christ. Good works are important but they are not sufficient for salvation. Righteousness can be honorable, but human righteousness is not good enough to merit salvation. Committing homicides and suicide to gain salvation is alien and diametrically opposed to Christianity. It is sinful pride for anyone to attempt to impose or enforce their self-righteousness on others. The sectarian and self-righteous are blind to their own sinfulness. They condemn others not realizing that they are under condemnation themselves. God declares that vengeance belongs to God.

3. <u>Individual and Group Salvation</u>

There are significant corporate benefits that accrue from Christian believers to non-Christian believers. Christians are taught to be concerned about the general welfare of society, and the common good of the community. It is God's Will for Christians to be a blessing to others.

The practice of Christian beliefs in group and communal settings, such as the home, school and other community groups, generates substantial goodwill, positive productivity and a healthy environment. Therefore, it can be easily concluded that the values and benefits go beyond the believers in Christ and impacts in a good way for the general community and the common good of all. America is a case in point. The Christian values and the Christian way of life in America for the past 400 years have been the enriching, civilizing, stabilizing and progressive positive force. Christianity has been the under girding foundation for the progress and success of America. Christmas is the most celebrated holiday in America and the most recognized throughout the earth. It goes without saying that God has overwhelmingly blessed America through Christianity. However, it must be pointed out that all persons who identify themselves as Christians, and many who even attend and have membership in churches have not accepted Jesus Christ as their Lord and Savior. Many people are benefiting from the social, political, educational and economic salvation derived from Christianity.

Group salvation, as has been discussed, is a significant component of Christianity. However, there is no substitute for individual personal salvation through belief and faith in Jesus Christ. Therefore, it is incumbent upon each individual to accept Jesus Christ as personal savior to receive the gift of eternal life. Parents cannot receive this gift for their children. Ministers cannot receive it for friends or spouses, or anyone else can receive the gift for anyone else. Each individual must make his own choice.

Believers in Christ have established friendships, partnerships, companionships and various other fellowships. However, God has so designed God's plan of salvation that each individual must make his or her own personal choice to accept or to reject Jesus Christ. Christianity is individual and corporate. It is built on a vertical individual relationship with God above and a horizontal outreach communal relationship with other individuals. This individual relationship with God through Jesus Christ is not intended to foster exclusion or individualistic self-centered living as a Christian. On the contrary, the believer in Christ gets involved and engaged in redemptive salvation services in the world society.

4. <u>Christianity and Evangelism</u>

Christians are commissioned to go into all the world with the gospel of Jesus Christ. It is to be carried forth by teaching, preaching, exhortation, proclamation and witnessing through benevolent services.

Jesus' disciples were never instructed to use physical force or any other aggressive means to get others to accept or believe the gospel. Forced acceptance to the gospel of Christ is alien to the spirit of Jesus Christ. Christian conversion cannot be forced. It results form the voluntary acceptance of Jesus as Lord and Savior. God gives the individual freedom of conscience, freedom of choice as an autonomous person. When a person is forced physically or through intimidation to conform to a prescribed behavior or pattern of thinking, amount to a gross violation of human dignity and unauthorized enslavement.

Jesus specifically instructed his disciples on one occasion, that if they are rejected during their missionary journey by a township or community, to leave the township or community and dust off their feet as they leave and proceed to another place. Jesus admonished his disciples on another occasion to not throw their pearls among swine. Swine do not have an appreciation for pearls. Swine will trample pearls in the mud and sometimes turn against the ones who are giving away the pearls.

These instructions and admonishments of Jesus to his disciples emphasizes that there is no intent on the part of the Christian to force or impose the gospel of Christ on any person. Additionally, there are no reprisals taken against those persons or groups who reject the gospel. Apostle Paul was the most zealous of the Christian missionaries and the most prolific writer of the church of Christ. He never advocated forced conversions in his missionary journeys or in the books that he wrote in the New Testament.

Hopefully, this brief discourse on Christianity and Evangelism will put to rest the uniformed false claims that Christians in America attempt to impose their religion and moral values on non-Christian believers. On the contrary, since there is a movement to de Christianize America, an investigation may reveal that the non believers in Christ are the culprits who are attempting to impose their anti Christian beliefs and values on the Christians in America.

5. Christianity and American Democracy
   Christians established the American Democratic form of government in America. The Declaration of Independence, the United States Constitution, the Pledge of Allegiance to the Flag, the motto, "In God We Trust," were written by Christians. The documents are based on Christian principles. The United States Constitution and the Amendments to the Constitution are closely allied with biblical

principles and Christian doctrines in the Holy Bible.

It is interesting and noteworthy that the First Amendment to the U. S. Constitution rules out a theocratic form of government. It vests the ultimate power in the people to be ruled by the consent of the governed. The U. S. Constitution prohibits dictatorial, theocratic, aristocratic or any other sectarian, special interest or factional rule. In view of the First Amendment, the U. S. Government must be diligent in regards to the wave of immigrants with their various political, religious and other belief systems. It would be unwise not to recognize early on for conflicting belief systems in the country that could precipitate constitutional and other national crises.

It must be emphasized as significant that Christianity and democracy have operated complementary and compatibly in America. Christianity and democracy have invited the world to America. The Statue of Liberty in New York City harbor symbolizes this invitation. The outstretched arms of America and the welcoming heart of the Christian believers in America have received people from all over the world. The foundation of this reception and accommodation rested on Christianity and democracy in America. It must be recognized that no other nation in history has achieved the level of prosperity as the United States of America. Therefore, Christianity and democracy have demonstrated a model of government to serve all people in freedom. God has truly blessed America.

6. Christian Challenges to U. S. Constitution

The enslavement and the subsequent racial discrimination of black people of African descent in America presented a Christian challenge to the

U. S. Government and the U. S. Constitution. This Christian challenge resulted in the issuance of the Emancipation Proclamation in 1863 and the 13th Amendment outlawing involuntary servitude in the United States in 1865.

Racial segregation and racial discrimination subsequent to slavery presented another landmark challenge to the U. S. Government and Constitution. The challenges of the 1960s were led by black American Christians. Dr. Martin Luther King, Jr. of the Southern Christian Leadership Conference spearheaded the Civil Rights Movement from 1955 to 1968 when he was assassinated.

This Christian challenge to the U. S. Government and the U. S. Constitution during the 1960s resulted in the 1964 and other Civil Rights legislation upholding the Fourteenth Amendment of the United States Constitution. There have been other Christian/legal challenges to the U. S. Constitution. They are labeled as Christians because the leadership of the Civil Rights Movement consisted of primarily black Christian ministers. It was a civil rights movement under girded by Christian principles.

The Civil Rights Movement was successful primarily because of the compatibility and kindred doctrines of the U. S. Constitution and Christian principles. The conflicts and contradictions of the segregation laws were forced to yield to justice, truth and righteousness of Christianity.

Christians have constituted the largest religious majority in the United States for over two hundred years. It is interesting and significant to note that there have not been any strong tendencies or expressions for a Christian theocracy in America. In spite of the large numbers of outstanding Christian pastors and Christian leaders, there has been hardly any notable interest of ministers seeking the U. S. presidency. The few ministers who have aspired to be U. S. presidents have not had Christian theocracy in mind. This highlights the fact that Christianity has a productive coexisting compatibility with democracy. It also highlights the fact that Christians have been very tolerant and extraordinarily accommodating to Protestants, Catholics, Jews, other religious groups, as well as other nationalities and cultures.

The practice of Christianity and democracy has not been perfect or even near perfection. There have been and continue to be many violations and many atrocities of civil rights. However, America with its largest religious majority of Christians, has afforded more opportunities and more acceptance to culturally diverse ad religious pluralistic people than any other nation in history.

The black Americans, the offspring of slaves, have struggled for civil rights and human dignity in America since 1619. It has been their belief in the Holy Bible and their faith in the God of Jesus Christ that compelled them to challenge the U. S. Government and Constitution. The Christian and legal victories that they have won have helped the nation and the world. The American Democracy and faith in Jesus Christ have opened up opportunities and kept hope alive for the black Americans.

American history is replete with its acceptance, tolerance and accommodations to the incoming immigrants with their various cultures and beliefs into a receptive predominant Christian nation. The question for the 21st Century is not whether America and Christianity will accept the new immigrants and other religions. The history of America and Christianity in America has already answered that question in the affirmative.

The questions that must be asked now are:
1. Will the immigrants and other religions accept America and Christianity without trying to impose their own imported limitations and values?

2. Is it safe for Americans and compatible with the U. S. Constitution to accept immigrants, religions and ideologies that are diametrically opposed to the cooperative and accommodative spirit of democracy?

Christianity and Other Religions

The increasing religious pluralism in America is putting those who identify themselves as Christians on the defensive. It is rapidly becoming socially prohibitive, politically and even theologically incorrect to use the name of Jesus Christ in the public domain.

Many Christians and even ministers of the Gospel feel that it is offensive to certain other religions to use the name of Jesus Christ in public and even in a Christian prayer. Christian ministers are even counseling and instructing other ministers to avoid using the name of Jesus or Christ in their prayers when they pray at public meetings.

Textbooks and other books are being written and published which no longer use BC (Before Christ) or AD, Anno domini (In the Year of Our Lord). To highlight the seriousness and extremity of this time line reference, there is a theological textbook used in theological seminaries, entitled, The Story of Christianity, which uses BCE (Before Common Era) instead of BC (Before Christ) and ACE (After Common Era) instead of AD (In the Year of our Lord).

If this is happening at the seminaries, it must be much more expansive at the secular publication level. This trend of eliminating the name of Jesus Christ in public places and eliminating it from publications and public documents is a serious matter that must be addressed. It is a blatant unethical and misrepresentative violation of historical facts and truth.

It is ironic that a Christian theologian objected to the use of the word, Christian, in the title of the organization, Christian Association of Public Theologians. He also objected to the word, Christian, in the title of the organization, Christian Institute of Public Theology. This person who claims to be an ordained minister with a doctorate in theology stated that the use of the word, Christian, is too exclusive. He stated that the word, Christian, excluded Jews, Muslims and persons of other faiths who would have an interest in public theology.

This particular theologian also made another interesting statement regarding a serious disadvantage in using the word, Christian, in the name of an organization. He stated that Christians must be mindful that in higher education the use of the name of one religion, such as Christianity, could have an adverse affect on accreditation and funding possibilities. It is enlightening to learn that the associations that determine what institutions qualify for accreditation and what institutions qualify for funding could disqualify or penalize a Christian organization or institution based on the use of its Christian name.

If this is the policy of the accreditation and funding institutions, a detailed rationale for such a policy is needed. The policy must be evaluated by public theology to determine whether the policy is valid and sound. Many public policies become established on the basis of unsound doctrines and faulty premises. Many policies with theological implications are made without any theological consult. Unsound policies can have damaging and negative consequences. It is extremely important that theology get involved in the exploring, evaluating and making public policy.

The questions must be asked and the issues must be raised as to who is making these decisions and what authority is being used to decide the appropriate, moral ethical and legal issues involved in certifications and accreditations. Can a Christian name of an organization or institution be used to conclude that it is exclusive of non-Christians? What is the meaning and definition of religious exclusivity if that is a prerequisite for certifications accreditations and qualifications?

It must be recognized that those who control accreditation, qualifications, certifications and funding wield substantial influence and power over organizational and institutional operations. Therefore, it is the obligation and sacred duty of the public theologian and the American government to assure that those who set policy for religious, educational and governmental organizations are duly

The Way out of Darkness

qualified, adequately informed with the factual truth and justly authorized by the appropriate authority.

The high rate of tolerance and accommodation for the large number of immigrating nationalities, races, ethnicities, cultures and religions by the American people and Christians continue to put Americans on the defensive. Americans are not just expected or required to tolerate and accommodate more and more differences, but the Americans are being asked to give up its patriotism as Americans and its identity as Christians.

This excessive tolerance and accommodation for the immigrants has put America up for grabs by the world. More and more immigrants and more illegal aliens express the feeling that they have a bonafide legitimate right to stake their claim on America without regard to those who have labored in America, enslaved in America, sacrificed and died for America.

Many immigrants and aliens come to America with total disregard for the black indigenous Americans who have never received their just benefits and compensations as Americans. This is not intended to cast any blame on the immigrants and aliens. Many are not aware of the history of the indigenous black Americans. However, many black Americans feel that immigrants and aliens have received more tolerance and more accommodations in America than they have.

It appears that the unbounded tolerance and accommodations of the newly arrived and arriving immigrants has eroded the American and Christian identities in America. It seems to have robbed them of their ability and will to be firm in their identities as Christians and Americans and to assert themselves as people and believers with a mission. The American Christians have become confused about their identity and responsibility and have lost focus of their mission.

The diminished identities of American Christians and the abandonment of mission have happened because the influx of diverse immigrants has compelled the American Christians to accommodate the identities and missions of the immigrants. This diluting and disabling encroachment has been allowed and reinforced because Christian Americans have been taught that it is both democratic and

Christian to tolerate and accommodate others. However, Christian Americans have not been taught well enough that your soul must not be sold or given away and that faith in Jesus Christ is non negotiable. The light of Christ must not be put out and his commission must not be compromised. One must hold on to his soul. Nothing must be allowed to get between your soul and your Savior. The duty of a Christian is to be a transforming agent in the world and not to be transformed by the world.

Inclusivity of Christianity: The Dilemma

The tolerant and accommodating attitudes and dispositions of Christians in a democratic society have caused a serious dilemma for the Christians. In a democratic society with the influx of diverse immigrants, the Christian feels that if her or she asserts him or herself as Christians, that this assertion will be offensive to the religious beliefs of others. Also, another part of this dilemma is, that when the Christian is tolerant of persons with non-Christian beliefs, a message is being sent to the non-Christian that his different religion is okay. When the message is sent to the non-Christian that his beliefs and religion are okay, negates the vitality of the Gospel of Jesus Christ. Can the Christian be true to Christ and belief in the Gospel by sending a message, verbally or through acquiescent silence, that the non-Christian's religion is okay?

This tolerance and accommodation of other religions by the Christian appear to be considerate, virtuous and charitable, as well as democratic. However, the Christian is caught in a serious dilemma. This dilemma has paralyzed and immobilized the Christian into neutrality, passivity and inaction. However, the longer this paralysis and immobility continue, the more serious the dilemma and the more corrosive and malignant the crisis grows.

Resolution to the Dilemma

The Way out of Darkness

Every person must know that Christianity is the most inclusive and most universal world religion. Christians embrace the Holy Bible from Genesis to Revelation. The Christians accept the Hebrew Bible, known as the Old Testament. Christians accept the New Testament as the fulfillment of the Old Testament.

The identity of Jesus Christ is confirmed by over a hundred prophecies in the Old Testament. The identity of Jesus, his life, his crucifixion and resurrection are historically confirmed by credible eyewitnesses and infallible proofs.

The resurrection of Jesus Christ is confirmed by the canonized Gospel of Matthew, Mark, Luke, and John, Peter, Paul, James and Jude. He is confirmed by his post resurrection words, the Great Commission and specific appearances. He is confirmed by the Holy Spirit on the Day of Pentecost. He is confirmed by the preaching of Peter and the conversion of Paul. He is confirmed by the new birth and the new creature. He is confirmed by the great cloud of witnesses that number in the billions. He is confirmed in the splitting of history into B. C. and A. D. He is confirmed by the voice of God, "This is my beloved Son in whom I am well pleased."

Christianity is not a mystical religion. It is not based on a dream, vision, fiction, or fantasy. It is concretely and spiritually rooted in history. It is factually, truthfully and reality based. Christianity embodies and incorporates the truth.

Who or what in the universe has enough knowledge, authority or power to refute the historical and revelatory truths of the Holy Bible and the unsearchable and inexhaustible riches of Jesus Christ? Where is the source of knowledge in all the annals of history that possess the validity to refute Jesus Christ? Name the person or thing under heaven that has the power or the authority to refute Jesus Christ.

The inexhaustible truths and riches of Jesus Christ provide more sustenance and resourcefulness than can ever be consumed by the Christian believer. The ultimate and absolute treasure is found in Jesus Christ. No comparable options exist.

The Ultimate Highest Ethical, Moral and Spiritual Values

The Christian can and must resolve his dilemma of moral paralysis and spiritual immobility due to the overly accommodation of other faiths and the acquiescence to his own. This dilemma can be resolved by recognizing and putting into perspective the vital optimum moral, ethical and spiritual values found in no other except Jesus Christ according to the Scriptures of the Holy Bible.

Consider what Christ offers and the alternatives:

In Christ we have:	Without Christ:
1. Life	Death
2. Love	Hatred
3. Truth	Deception
4. Righteousness	Wrong
5. Peace	Turmoil
6. Hope	Despair
7. Goodness	Evil
8. Beauty	Ugly
9. Light	Darkness
10. Mercy	Cruelty
11. Compassion	Indifference
12. Forgiveness	Vengeance
13. Justice	Injustice
14. Power	Impotence
15. Healing	Deterioration
16. Knowledge	Ignorance
17. Wisdom	Foolishness
18. Authority	Chaos

19. Sacrifice	Indulgence
20. Food	Starvation
21. Restoration	Separation
22. Reconciliation	Alienation
23. Holiness	Blasphemy
24. Reward	Punishment
25. Humility	Arrogance
26. Resurrection	Damnation
27. Freedom	Bondage
28. Rebirth	Death
29. Found	Lost
30. Sight	Blind
31. Eternity	Limited Time
32. Understanding	Confusion
33. Advocate	Unrepresented

It is totally unreasonable and totally insane for anyone to forfeit or reject the life that is found in Christ. Life in Christ is the best bargain and the most precious gift in the whole world. No one in his right mind or right spirit would forfeit or reject Jesus. The alternative is total destruction. In Christ there is everything to gain. Without Christ there is everything to lose.

No individuals or groups have a monopoly on Christ. The invitation of Jesus Christ is to the whole world. The invitation of Christianity is to the whole world. There is no force and no violence in his invitation. It is an invitation of love. He knocks tenderly on the door of the heart. He does not knock the door down.

The Gospel of Jesus Christ is good news. The Christian has a duty to spread this good news. Therefore, only those who reject this good news are offended. In reality, the good news of Christ is not offensive to them. They are offensive to the good news. Those who reject Christ are the ones who are exclusive and intolerant and non-accommodating. Only an antichrist spirit could be offended by the Gospel of Christ. Christians have no duty to tolerate and accommodate antichrist spirits.

The Christian role in a pluralistic world is not to criticize or condemn other religions. The Christian role is to take the message to them or provide the message to them or provide the message for them when they are in the midst. The Christian must go forward, uninhibited, proactively and rationally with the message of Christ.

It must be remembered that the antichrist spirit is also anti truth, anti love, anti light, anti life, anti freedom and anti God. It is irrational, self destructive, self defeating and suicidal to tolerate and accommodate the antichrists at the expense of the universal and all-inclusive Gospel for all people. The dilemma is resolved. Be obedient to God and loyal to the worldwide mission of Christ.

Christianity and Globalization

Jesus was born a Jew in the lineage of David, the greatest king of Israel about one thousand years after the life of David. Therefore, Christianity was born in Judaism. Jesus extended his Gospel beyond Judaism into all the world. Therefore, the Gospel of Christ was global long before the concept of globalization was born.

The Gospel of Christ is designed for all people throughout the earth. Globalization through modern technology has brought the peoples of the world into a closer and more intimate contact than ever before. Although, globalization as it is known today was not imagined two thousand years ago. However, the Gospel of Christ offers the only hope of survival by the crisis precipitated by globalization. The geographical and technological coming together of the different peoples of the world is creating tension, confusion, conflicts and wars. Cultures, religions, belief systems, customs and ideas are conflicting and clashing. There is hope for peace and unity in the universal and inclusive Gospel of Jesus Christ. Christianity is a citadel of hope, love and goodwill.

Christianity transcends racism, ethnocentrism, sexism, sectarianism, regionalism, culturalism, classism, nationalism, patriotism, cultism, mysticism, legalism and paternalism. Christianity offers an atmosphere of freedom, autonomy and democracy for all people.

Christianity does not impose arbitrary standards. It allows for and encourages the optimum self-actualization of all people to live in harmony and for the common good and to the glory of God. Christianity is not a religion of oppression and suppression. It is a true religion of liberation, healing, restoration, forgiveness and mercy. Jesus Christ is the only one qualified to lead the awesome diversity existing in a technological, fragmented globalized world. This does not mean that other religions do not have something of value to offer. Christianity has the complete package.

Christianity and God

The Holy Bible is the primary authority on the revelation, nature, works and Will of God. It has over four thousand years of written documentation of God's revelation from above and man's discovery from below. The Bible tells the story of God's revelation to reach and redeem humankind on the earth. It is a revelation of God's acts and interventions in history.

The Old Testament is an account of God's acts and interactions with the people of Israel. God's reach for man did not stop with the people of Israel. Jesus Christ became the most complete revelation and self-disclosure of God. St. John declares that Jesus was the Word in the beginning with God and that the Word became flesh and dwelt among us. Jesus told his followers that no man has seen God at any time. He told them further, "If you have seen me, you have seen the Father."

In 325 A. D. at the Council of Nicea, the church fathers declared that Jesus Christ is coequal and coeternal with God, the Father. The decision was confirmed at the Council of Constantinople in 381 A. D. At the Synod of Rome in 382 A. D. the New Testament canon was accepted in the West. At the Synod of Carthage in 397

A. D. the New Testament canon was accepted by the entire church. The New Testament documents the life and ministry of Jesus Christ, the most celebrated event of all history.

Jesus Christ is unique in history. No other individual has been elevated and exalted to the heavens as Jesus Christ. He is exalted to the bosom of the Triune God. Jesus makes the claim that he is the Door Way to God. The Door is open to all humanity. In the past two thousand years, billions of people have entered that Door. It is done by individual choice. For those who choose not to enter must not be allowed to hinder or block the Door Way for others who wish to enter.

CHAPTER 11

Guides for Ethical Decisions

Rationale for Ethical Decisions

Ethical decisions are vital for the well being of individuals as well as for the security and well being of society. The decisions that individuals make, as well as corporate groups, determines success or failure in many instances, as well as life and death. Decision-making ranges from bad to good. Bad decisions often cause great harm and costly damages to self and others. Many are not just costly, but also fatal and catastrophic.

A bad decision or an unethical decision does not always mean that the person making such a decision is bad. Well-meaning and well-intentioned people often make bad decisions. A bad decision can have negative and even lethal consequences in spite of its good intentions. Since decision-making is so critically important, it is essential to explore and analyze the decision-making process in order to provide some guidance to assist individuals and corporate bodies to make the best and most ethical decisions possible.

Primary Reasons for Bad Decisions

1. Bad Intentions
   It is clear that when individuals plan, connive, conspire and strategize to do harm to others, this can be considered in many cases, illegal, unlawful, and of course unethical. Decisions that violate the personal, human and civil rights of others constitute bad decisions. There is an adjudicatory process in the courts to litigate and dispose of such violations.

2. Incompetence and Lack of Knowledge
   Bad decisions are often made due to incompetence and a lack of knowledge. The responsible and good decision-maker must have a fund of knowledge and experience commensurate with the decision to be made. Decisions made in ignorance and darkness are usually bad and inappropriate decisions. It is suggested that increased knowledge, education and spiritual enlightenment have the potential to improve good decision-making. This is especially important where corporate and political decisions are made. Good decision-making capability must be a major consideration for those persons who aspire, appointed or who otherwise assume leadership positions in the society.

3. Arbitrary and Random Choices
   Arbitrary and random decisions have no consideration for reality or rationality regarding values, priorities or consequences regarding the decision. An arbitrary decision is a blind and insensitive decision. Arbitrary and random decisions fail to evaluate, analyze and employ ethical and moral considerations. An arbitrary decision is analogous to blind folding one's self and pulling available selections out of the hat. The

random decision-maker presumes that one decision or selection is as good as the other. It is worse than flipping a coin, because the coin has only two choices, head or tail. Usually, there are many more choices in the complex decisions of life. God has given man and woman an intellect, a mind, to store knowledge and make rational decisions based on divine standards, righteousness, truth, justice and love. When the established standards of God are ignored in human decision-making, the consequences are costly and damaging to the decision-maker and society.

4. <u>Irresponsibility</u>
Bad decisions are often made due to irresponsibility. People who are irresponsible are often immature with a lack of focus, alertness and seriousness regarding the issues at hand. Individuals who are irresponsible cannot be depended on to carry out instructions, follow policies and procedures or make sound judgments. Irresponsible individuals usually have their minds, interest and energies focused in many different directions. Irresponsibility is often rooted in childish and immature behavior. We must not depend on children to be responsible for making good, sound and dependable decisions. There is a need to include in the American educational curriculum courses that will encourage maturity, sound judgment and responsibility, as well as accountability.

5. <u>External Influences</u>
Many individuals are influenced by other persons and situations to make bad decisions. Political considerations play a major role in decision-making. Many decision makers make choices based on what pleases certain persons and certain constituents. Peer pressures influence decisions. Some decisions are bought and some decisions are sold. Factors

of bargaining, negotiating, accommodating, compromising, profiting and greed frequently contribute to bad decisions. External influences have significant impact on decision-making.

6. <u>Perception Distortion Through Emotional Trauma</u>
Emotional and psycho-traumatic experiences can trigger bad decisions. The emotional and mental status can be a major factor in decision-making. We must be aware as to how anger, anxiety, depression, disappointment, loneliness, heart break, feelings of rejection and injustice, as well as fear can affect decision making. This suggests very strongly that the mental, emotional, physical and spiritual health of decision makers must be taken into consideration and in many instances must be monitored. In the case of corporate leaders who make decisions for large numbers of people, we must be sure that effective checks and balances are in place. The stakes are too high and the cost is too expensive to risk isolated decision-making. Overall health is a significant factor.

7. <u>Drug Induced Judgment Impairment</u>
It is common knowledge that drug use, drug abuse and drug addiction are rampant and extensive in the American society. The DSM-IV (The Diagnostic Statistical Manual, Volume IV) enumerates the symptoms, effects, withdrawal syndrome and other induced effects of drug use and abuse. The DSM-IV is published by the American Psychiatric Association. It is a volume that lists all of the mental and emotional disorders. A substantial number of mental and emotional illnesses are induced by the use and abuse of alcohol and other drugs. The vast majority of persons under the jurisdiction of the criminal justice system are there because of use and association with alcohol and other drugs. The illicit and sometimes licit mind

altering drugs result in significant impairment of judgment of persons under the influence of these drugs. The impairment of thinking ability and judgment capacity is not limited to just the illicit drugs or just to persons in the criminal justice system and the mental institutions. There are many persons in society who have not been arrested or referred for substance abuse or mental health services who are impaired mentally, and emotionally. There is also a significant number of impaired professionals. These impaired professionals are in all segments of society. They include medical and other health professionals, lawyers, clergy, public officials and other community leaders. Many of these persons and professionals are functioning in their various positions. However, their decision-making capacities are significantly diminished because of alcohol and other drug use and abuse. Because of this bad decisions are often made.

Conclusions

One important positive thing can be concluded from these seven reasons behind bad decisions. That one positive is, that, there is a rational reason behind bad decision-making, and these seven reasons for bad decision-making can be rationally and systematically corrected. There is also an urgency that requires that the corrections begin without delay. Bad decisions are too costly and threatening to civilization. The consequences of our individual and corporate bad decisions have already created an overwhelming deficit in our God given human potential. Therefore it is mandatory to correct our faulty decision-making behavior and immediately establish priorities to make good decisions and the best and most positive and beneficial decisions possible. Bad decisions hurt. Bad decisions kill. Bad decisions are against humanity.

__Christian Ethics in Decision-making__

Christian ethics enables the serious minded person to arrive at the more precise, objective, true and right decision in matters of moral and ethical conclusions. Christian ethics is critical in avoiding arbitrary, biased and subjectively judgmental decisions. The Holy Bible is the universal authority on ethics, morality, religion and all laws that govern the conduct and character of human nature and human behavior.

Globalization requires that moral and ethical decisions be made on the basis of universal principles and universal values. This is the only hope for peace and survival in a world that is rapidly becoming international, culturally diverse and religiously pluralistic. Localism, privitism and sectarianism must open up to accommodate and accept universalism. The irreconcilable differences in localism, privitism and sectarianism are fraught with competition, conflict, disharmony and war. Their selfish goals, self centered interests and limited concerns keep them in a state of perpetual friction, conflict and self-defeating negations. The destruction of civilization has been made possible through the development of scientific technology. Therefore it is a human survival necessity to overcome ideologies of cultism and sectarianism.

The divisive problems of cultism, sectarianism and idolatry are very old. For thousands of years these ideological differences and idolatrous allegiances did not pose the threat level that they pose in the last 60 years. Technology has made the difference within the past one hundred years. This means that our ideological differences and conflicts can be translated into computerized global nuclear warfare.

> The Holy Scriptures have warned about the separations, alienations and turning away from the truth. Isaiah says, "All we like sheep have gone astray; we have turned everyone to his own way; and the Lord hath laid on Him the iniquity of us all." (Isaiah 53:6 KJV)

"There is a way which seemeth right unto man, but the end thereof are the ways of death." (Proverbs 14:12)

"The way of a fool is right in his own eyes, but he that hearkeneth to counsel is wise." (Proverbs 12:15)

"For I bear them record that they have a zeal of God, but not according to knowledge. For they being ignorant of God's righteousness, and going about to establish their own righteousness have not submitted themselves unto the righteousness of God." (Romans 10:2-3)

"Now the Spirit speaketh expressly, that in the latter times some shall depart from the faith, giving heed to seducing spirits, and doctrines of devils." (1Timothy 4:1)

"For the time will come when they will not endure sound doctrine, but after their own lusts shall they heap themselves teachers, having itching ears. And they shall turn away their ears from the truth, and shall be turned unto fables." (2Timothy 4:3-4)

"For the Lord knoweth the way of the righteous: but the way of the ungodly shall perish." (Psalm 1:6)

"Where there is no vision, the people perish." (Proverbs 29:18)

"My people are destroyed for lack of knowledge; because thou hast rejected knowledge, I will also reject thee." (Hosea 4:6)

It is significant to know that the above scriptures were written over two thousand years ago. They were written before mankind had conceived of automobiles, airplanes, the telephone, computers or nuclear weapons. And yet, the Scriptures describe the core problem of this advanced unique nuclear age. The Scriptures also provide the answers and solutions for the complex dire problems of this nuclear age.

The core problem of this civilization threatened nuclear age is an ethical problem. Therefore, we must elevate ethics as a priority and begin to major in the education and the practice of ethical behavior.

Enforce Professional Ethics

Why must professional ethics be enforced? Professional ethics must be enforced rigorously because the professionals make the policies, procedures, bureaucracies, guidelines, qualifications and allocations for services to the public. Professional ethics suggests competence, fairness, respect for human dignity and a demonstrated commitment for the common good.

There is evidence in the American society that professionalism and professional ethics are deteriorating in our agencies, institutions, professions, corporations, businesses and the society in general. The efficiency, dependability, fairness and quality of resources and services are in serious decline. This decline of professionalism and professional ethics are not limited to the secular world. It includes the religious and educational institutions as well. The decline of ethical considerations in a society is a clear sign of moral and spiritual decay.

The decline of professional ethics has the effect of violating and assaulting human dignity. It decreases quality of life and sometimes destroys life itself. Unethical and unprofessional conduct hurts life. It causes great stress and substantial inconveniences. Unethical and unprofessional conduct contributes to low self esteem and feelings of unworthiness. Over a period of time of being subjected to perpetrators or unprofessionalism, one can become demoralized. Demoralization is a wounded spirit. Wounded spirits often bring about discouragement and depression.

Professional ethics must be enforced because unethical and unprofessional behavior practiced on other people does real harm and real damage to the health and well being of such victimized people. The harmful effects of unethical behavior is under estimated and often undetected by casual observers because of the passive nature or the insidious nature of the unethical or unprofessional behavior. Unprofessional and unethical are being used synonymously in this discussion because I believe it is unethical to be unprofessional and unprofessional to be unethical.

It is unethical and unprofessional to be discourteous and unkind to persons who present themselves as invitees to your public service or public business. Businesses have a duty to be courteous and kind to their customers. Discourtesy and unkindness are insults to our customers and clients. It is offensive and personally assaulting to address clients and customers in an unfriendly or hostile tone of voice. Also, it is not just the tone of voice that can be offensive and painful, but also demeaning and arrogant looks and gestures can be very offensive to clients and customers. The eyes, the face, the hands, the body and the walk can be used to convey hateful and negating messages. Body language can be a powerful force to make clients and customers feel bad.

Clients, customers and associates are personally disregarded in many ways. They are often kept waiting extensively for service without any explanation. The time and schedule of clients and customers are totally disregarded. Too often, there is no consideration for time, schedule and transportation inconveniences.

Too often, clients and customers are not provided clear instructions or directions on paper or geographical directions as to how to locate certain services or places are very poor. The labeling of buildings, parking lots and the interior labels are very poor or non-existent. In most buildings, the halls, elevators, floors and doors for various services are woefully deficient. There is great need for labeling addresses and making the numbers and street names visible and street names visible so they can be seen day or night.

There is a great need in making the labels of floors, elevators, parking lots, restrooms, service rooms and exits more graphically visible. It is inconsiderate, insensitive and unethical to fail to provide essential information for clients knowing where they are and having signs to point clearly where they need to go. Providing these simple instructions and appropriate designated labeling can reduce a substantial amount of stress and unnecessary anxiety. This is sufficiently important to be mandated by law under public accommodation. This is especially needed for the elderly and others who are physically and otherwise challenged.

More increasingly, it is becoming difficult to speak with a person as opposed to automated telephone service. In too many instances automated services are not sufficient or appropriate to meet the needs of many clients and customers. It is often excessively time consuming and stressful to deal with automated services and voice mail messages. There is no adequate substitute for a human being in the business transaction process. Machines can often be efficient, but they are devoid of the human quality to be kind, considerate and courteous. It is unethical to allow automated machines to replace human beings.

In the course of business enterprise, professional and ethical safeguards must be in place to protect the public from arbitrary, discriminatory and capricious attitudes and actions. It is well known that some of the customer service representatives and some of the client service providers have judgmental, prejudicial and antagonistic predispositions. It is also well known that many persons who are entrusted with authority and responsibility to work with the public and those persons who are fragile and vulnerable are not always suitable or qualified. Many people use their positions and authority to unleash their bitterness and frustrations onto especially the poor and the disadvantaged. There are persons with toxic personalities who ventilate their negative feelings to others and contribute to the creation of hostile work and living environments. There is no adequate measure for the extensive pain and damage created by the hostile persons and hostile environments. However, the damages and dysfunctions are too extensive and expensive to be left alone without some form of intervention.

It is the responsibility of public theology through the means of professionalism and professional ethics to create safe atmospheres, safe environments and safe places for the human spirits to exist and interact in peace with respect and dignity. This can be done through proper education, training, guidelines, policies and procedures. There is no need for the continuation of misguided ventilations and intimidations. The problem can be fixed. The self-defeating and self-destructive problems must be fixed. The health of the nation and the safety of the world require it. The promotion of professionalism and ethical values in our places of work and commerce will enrich, strengthen and add unity and increase prosperity, peace and patriotism.

The resources and the leadership of public theology are available to guide this revolutionary process of promoting and teaching professionalism, ethical values and character development.

Professional Ethics

The practice of public theology must rest firmly on professional ethics. Professional ethics is a basic requirement for all agents and agencies that do business or provide services to persons in the private or public domain. The human dignity of every person must be respected at all times. There must not be any transgressions or violations of any person, their property rights or their civil or human rights.

It must be recognized that personal, property and human rights violations can do irreparable harm to the reputation and credibility of perpetrating individuals and agencies. Such violations can cause disruption in the delivery of human services, personal damage, liabilities, lawsuits, and loss of job, certifications and licensure.

Unprofessional conduct has caused many persons to lose the privilege of working with the clients and customers of their profession. This unfortunate loss of opportunity and privilege to work as a human services provider due to unethical violations can be very traumatic with long lasting adverse consequences and ramifications. It is an ongoing challenge of the business world, as well as the church to encourage the training and the professional ethical development of ministers, laity and other human services providers to observe and practice the highest codes of professional ethics.

The observance and practice of professional ethics is the minimum standard of operation for public theology. Professionalism is a vital requirement for providing human services, as well as conducting business and relating to individuals and agencies form all walks of life. When a business or agency fails to measure up to acceptable standards of conduct and ethical business practices, it is a major turn off for most people. Unethical and unprofessional practices can disqualify an agency from doing business and the credentials for doing business can be revoked.

Professionalism Is Good for Business

Professionalism promotes good business and good health. A professional and ethically operated business is efficient, productive, healthy and self-promoting. When people receive good services in a professional and efficient manner, they are likely to spread the good news to others. When individuals receive optimum benefits and minimum cost in their business and service transactions, they feel good. A good feeling in such an encounter is a health benefit. This health benefit can be multiplied. The promotion of professional and ethical practices in organizational and business enterprises can add significantly to the health of the nation.

Four Essential Elements of Professionalism

1. The professional must subscribe to and operate upon a recognized body of knowledge. This knowledge must be tested, or capable of being tested and validated to be factual, true and sound knowledge. It must be universally recognized as scientific, artistic, ethical or theological knowledge. This recognized body of knowledge must meet the sufficient and appropriate standards for the professional services to be provided. This recognized body of knowledge required by professionals must be from a bonafide established authoritative source. True factual bonafide validated knowledge existing in a reality based historical

context is distinguished from fictions, fantasies, dreams, imagination, visions, mysticism.

2. Professionalism requires a proficient and functional level of competence. The leader, teacher, service provider, administrator, bureaucrat or executive must be qualified with the sufficient education/training and appropriate certification, licensure and/or the acceptable and sufficient credential standard to provide the respective service or perform the respective job. The professional must possess the qualifications, knowledge and skills to perform the job or service at hand. The professional practitioner must have skills beyond guesswork or trial and error. He or she must be able to do the job or perform the service better than anyone else.

3. Professionalism requires subscription to a benevolent code of ethics. A benevolent code of ethics incorporates fairness, honesty, respect, and humane and dignified standards of conduct. Benevolence suggests that the clients and consumers of service will not be knowingly harmed or hindered. Furthermore, all efforts will be used to help and enhance the welfare of the client/consumer. A benevolent code of ethics prohibits any form of dishonesty, fraudulent or exploitative behavior.

4. Professionalism requires a concern for and an investment in the common good of society. Professional services which take place within the society, must operate in the best interest of society. Consumers of professional services are members of society and their well-being is connected with the well being of society. Therefore, the professional must have a manifested concern for society in conjunction with the welfare of the client or consumer who is a

member of society. A professional who does not care about the welfare of society cannot have a bonafide concern for the clients or consumers entrusted to his/her care. Clients and consumers of service, as well as the professional service provider, do not live in a vacuum, but in an interdependent society.

Public theology must promote holistic health in society. Holistic health can best be promoted by promoting professionalism and professional ethics. Professionalism and professional ethics have the potential to revolutionize the holistic health of the nation and enhance significantly the quality of life in America.

The serious practice and promotion of professional ethics will enrich the nation and its people with renewed energy and purpose. It will reduce selfishness and greed. It will stimulate motivation for education and self help. It will be an incentive to believe in noble ideals and values. It will inspire a drive for excellence. It will inspire a faith in God who can reveal to us that new heaven and new earth.

Willie James Webb

GUIDES FOR ETHICAL DECISIONS

Criteria for Ethical Decision-making

There are many elements involved in arriving at an ethical decision. It is not always simple to make a good ethical decision. A good ethical decision often requires a thorough study and evaluation of the situation at hand. It may also require personal soul searching and self- introspection and reflection because sometimes things are not seen objectively as they are, but rather subjectively as we are. Therefore, we must acknowledge our own biases and "baggage" that could enter into the decision in a negative way.

There are a number of pitfalls that we must be aware of as we endeavor to make ethical decisions.

1. One-sided decisions must be avoided. It is important to see all sides and the total picture in order to make the best ethical decision.

2. Avoid prejudgments and premature conclusions. Make a diligent effort to get all of the relevant available facts before rendering a decision.

3. Avoid the zeal and emotional fervor of self-righteousness. One can be right in his own sight and by his own standards, but not according to the

righteousness of God or the standards of God. A person can be sincerely wrong.

4. Where there is insufficient evidence, be willing to withhold judgment in abeyance of additional information.

5. Remember that we know in part and we see through a glass darkly. We depend on convincing and preponderance of evidence. Only God is absolute and omniscient. Therefore, when making ethical decisions, the theological perspective is indispensable. The theological perspective acknowledges the Will and power of God.

Ethical Evaluation Components

Twenty ethical evaluation components are listed below. Each component is put in the form of a question. Each question can be answered with yes, no, uncertain, along with biblical references for affirmation. It must be noted that some situations are not decisive enough to be answered with an unqualified yes or no. Some of the questions may call for an uncertain answer. Some of the questions may have a clear scriptural reference and some may not. Your conclusive answer may depend on the number of yes answers as opposed to the number of no answers. At least, the ethical evaluation components will require thought and consideration before arriving at an answer. And in some cases it will require some soul searching. This process of rationality and soul searching for ethical decisions will most certainly minimize, if not eliminate, random and arbitrary ethical decisions.

Willie James Webb

Criteria for Ethical Decision-making

Ethical Evaluation Components	Yes	No	Uncertain	Scriptural Reference
1. Is the decision right?	___	___	___	___
2. Is it legal?	___	___	___	___
3. Is it moral?	___	___	___	___
4. Is it fair/just?	___	___	___	___
5. Is it true?	___	___	___	___
6. Is it valid?	___	___	___	___
7. Is it justified?	___	___	___	___
8. Is it timely?	___	___	___	___
9. Is it urgent?	___	___	___	___
10. Is it essential?	___	___	___	___
11. Is it expedient?	___	___	___	___
12. Will cost Increase with delay?	___	___	___	___
13. Does it enhance life?	___	___	___	___
14. Is there redemptive value?	___	___	___	___
15. Is it wise?	___	___	___	___
16. Is it humane?	___	___	___	___
17. Is it merciful?	___	___	___	___
18. Is it loving?	___	___	___	___
19. Is it the Will of God?	___	___	___	___
20. Your biblical authority?	___	___	___	___
TOTALS	___	___	___	___

My Conclusion is _____

Based on the number of answers: Yes _____ No _____ Uncertain _____

Christian Institute of Public Theology, 2007 W. J. Webb

Summary

Ethical decision-making is not a simple process. It has been made more difficult by the advances in technology, the clashing of cultures, customs and ideologies, along with the corrosion of the traditional moral and ethical values. Therefore, it is the challenge of the public theologian to establish a rational procedure for arriving at the best ethical decision possible.

It is felt that this model featuring ethical evaluation components would provide some help in reaching an ethical decision through a rational and practical approach. It is felt that all of these components have been used by the conscientious ethicists. I have enumerated them so that they can be taught and applied more broadly. Some people are gifted with the knowledge, the wisdom and understanding to make ethical decisions. However, for those who are not so gifted, the criteria for ethical decision-making will be helpful. Ethical decision-making must not be based on fictions, fantasies, illusions, moral neutrality or random and arbitrary selections. There is an urgency for accuracy and precision in ethical decision-making. There is a high and predictable correlation between unethical decisions and detrimental consequences. There is such a high saturation of detrimental consequences because of unethical decisions that society must begin to reduce the looming dangers that unethical decisions create.

This is a call to all people to begin to place a top priority on ethical decision-making. Ethics in decision-making must be placed in our educational curricula at all levels. Because there is a significant difference between what is right and what is wrong; what is good and what is evil; what is just and what is unjust; what is love and what is hatred; what is light and what is darkness; what is true and what is false; what is life and what is death.

Ethical standards have been set for all people. Those who know those standards must practice them and teach others. Life and death or life or death is determined by individual and group decisions. Choose obedience to God and live.

Chapter 12

The Therapy of Worship

The excessive use of religion as private, individual and group therapy, contributes to the retreat of religion from the public domain. The function of religion as a therapeutic vehicle can be and often is a positive function of religion. Religion has a function of healing the brokenhearted, soothing pain, relieving stress and providing comfort and assurance to those who have been rejected and abused. It is commendable that a church worship service can be so rich and inspiring with its music, meditation prayers and message that parishioners will be healed and consoled. Thousands and perhaps millions come to church Sunday after Sunday to hear the joyful noise, message of hope and experience a fellowship of acceptance.

Social Problems Compel Worship

It is a great fortune and a worthwhile benefit for the church to serve as a refuge from the increasing social problems in a growing complex and stressful society. It can be a place to find at least a temporary escape from the problems and dangers from the outside world.

However, the more the church retreats and withdraws from the outside world, the problems and dangers are likely to increase.

Moral decadence, spiritual illness and unethical practices are a breeding ground for injustice and crime. Such conditions cannot be successfully retreated from. The retreat from the evil does not blot out the existence of the evil or its threat to destroy the total enterprise of the church and its values.

There is an increased demand for therapy for people who live in a stressful society and for people who have been abused by the injurious circumstances of life. Had it not been for the therapeutic function of the black church, it would have been acutely more difficult for black survival in America.

The black church was the primary institution that kept black people psychologically and spiritually alive. When they retreated from the hostilities of the outside world and took refuge in the churches on Sunday, sorrows were soothed, burdens were lifted, and minds were renewed. Hope was revived. This intermittent relief enabled them to keep on striving and to keep on living.

Black Americans, due to the tragic history of slavery and the persisting vestigial remnants of injustice continue to require an inordinate amount of therapy. The church worship experience provides some. The church does not always provide this therapy adequately. Because some churches have problems that precipitate the need for therapy within the church itself. Some unfortunate hurtful church experiences can present mental, physical and spiritual health hazards. This is to acknowledge that problems of the world often get into the church.

Too, often, the church is not effective in meeting the therapeutic needs of its members because the church is not aware of these needs. Most churches do not have specific social service programs in place with qualified personnel to provide the needed therapy for the masses of abused and neglected individuals in our society. An effective therapeutic program would be a program that would treat the problems and channel the energy and human resources into a more constructive use. An effective therapy would be to use the retreat therapy for renewal, recommitment and re-involvement. This will receive more elaboration as we continue on the subject, the invitation of public theology.

This need for therapy or this need for treatment and healing are basic motivations for much of the counterproductive and dysfunctional behavior that take place in the American society. There is perhaps, a larger number of people who do not go to church and who do not receive the benefit of the religious therapy provided by the church. This need for therapy is a driving force behind addictive, violent, anti social and criminal behavior. People who need therapy search for avenues to express their bad feelings and also to decrease or eliminate their bad feelings. Unfortunately, many people who feel bad, angry, resentful, rejected, neglected, abused, etc. will act out these bad feelings in negative and sometimes destructive and even self-destructive ways. People frequently involve themselves in risky, hazardous and bizarre behaviors in an effort to rid themselves of bad and/or negative feelings.

The energy, time and resources used to overcome bad feelings are very often counterproductive and in the long term create and compound the already existing bad feelings. The bad feelings go from bad to worse. The consumption of alcohol, drug abuse, profane expressions, negative attitudes, aggressive behavior have the net effects of increasing costs, damages, injuries and compounding the bad feelings. The need for therapy, therefore, is escalated to the need for crisis intervention, crisis stabilization, emergency and other remedial and other restorative services.

A primary problem with these misdirected needs for therapy is that the behavior is inner directed, selfishly motivated and blindly led. This means that there is a loss of focus on the outside world and the broader society. The common good for the community has been lost. The vast and disproportionate use of time, energy and resources are caught up in a vicious cycle of self-centeredness and self-gratification. This vicious cycle becomes an isolated and ineffective entity out of touch with the world of reality. This need for therapy is very pervasive. It is an issue addressed by public theology.

A More Constructive Therapy

Now that we are aware of the great need for therapy for a large number of people who live with pain and psychological trauma, it is a priority to begin to provide this urgent therapeutic need. The church has the potential to provide this therapy more appropriately and on a larger scale than any other institution. Among other functions, the church is an institution of healing. It has the facilities and the human resources. The church needs the will and the motivation to establish ongoing programs of practical and creative therapy for the many individuals who are in need. This does not mean that it is practical for each and every individual church to have such a program. In some instances groups of churches could sponsor joint programs for therapeutic treatment. In this same fashion, individual churches or groups of churches could sponsor the training of qualified, certified skilled therapeutic leaders.

Practical Therapy

Practical therapy is the creation of a safe non-threatening and congenial environment where a person can express and share negative and hurtful feelings in such a way that lead to healing and constructive behavior. The need for therapy is the need for regulated, guided, channeled emotional and mental expression for the relief of discomfort and pain. It is a need to regain emotional, mental and spiritual equilibrium.

Thoughts, feelings and morale can become destabilized and out of balance to the extent where normal functioning is disrupted and out of kilter. The brain and the psyche can become overly stimulated with psychic and emotional energy, as well as under stimulated. This out of kilter psychic energy can enrage a person to commit such violent acts as homicides and suicides. It can cause such confusion that the traumatized person may not know what to do and become psychologically paralyzed and behaviorally immobilized. It can also cause a person to feel spiritually defeated where the person loses hope, gives up and withers away. These various states of painful trauma have the potential for significant losses, damages, violations, addictions, abuses and tragedies.

Practical therapy offers great hope and unlimited opportunity for healing, healthy and constructive living. Practical therapy as opposed to traditional (medical model) therapy is less expensive, less stigmatizing and the services can be provided on a much wider scale. The traditional medical model therapy requires some type of psychiatric diagnosis. This usually involves a code number from the DSM IV (Diagnostic Statistical Manual IV) published by the American Psychiatric Association. It is obvious without going into lengthy details that traditional therapy is cost prohibitive, socially stigmatizing with limited affordability and availability. Traditional therapy also involves gathering a lot of personal and confidential information that can also be damaging when confidentiality is breached. Another great disadvantage of traditional therapy is that it is applied as a remedial service. It is provided when the therapeutic need has progressed to the point of needing crisis intervention, crisis stabilizations or downright life-threatening emergency intervention. Traditional therapy is limited in providing preventive and growth services; whereas, practical therapy is designed to specialize in preventive and growth services.

Premises of Practical Therapy

1. Most people at risk for mental illness, violence, drug abuse, dropping out of school, the labor market committing crimes, and resorting to other deviant behavior and deprived conditions can be helped significantly through practical therapy.

2. There are practical things that can be done to help people without the indulgence and superfluous use of the traditional means of treatment. In other words, if a practical solution will solve the problem, traditional solutions are abused and over used. For example, if a person is depressed and angry because he does not have money or employment, the traditional psychiatric referrals for intake, evaluation, diagnosis, assessment and prescribed medication for depression and counseling for anger management, by passes practical therapy. Practical therapy would assist the

person with employment and other legitimate ways of earning money and to use the energy generated by the anger, to do constructive activities.

3. People want to help themselves. They want to be involved in helping themselves. People sometimes get stuck between "a rock and hard place." Sometimes, they do not know how to overcome certain impasses and dilemmas. The injection or ingestion of medications into their systems really do not involve them or empower them to overcome their problems. Frequently, the side effects of the medication does more harm than good.

4. Most individuals who are in need of some form of help will respond more positively to a pleasant non-threatening environment and to helpers who are credentialed and validated as being competent, ethical and compassionate. Certified Public Theologians are presumed to have these qualifications as skilled helpers in practical therapy. It is critical that persons who are injured, damaged or otherwise victimized be assured that the helping environment and the prospective helpers themselves be safe, trustworthy and unconditionally caring and will not deceive or do further injure to the already victimized persons. The confidence, faith, trust and hope in the trustworthy, safe, professional and caring environment is a significant part of the healing process. The Certified Public Theologians are the skilled helpers to create and be a part of this healing and health promotion environment and process.

5. The church is designed and commissioned to establish, provide and promote practical therapy. It has the facilities, the human resources, the principles and the sound doctrines.

6. The church is the primary place and the largest institution for human healing in the American society. The overwhelming majority of pastors and church leaders will support practical therapy led by certified public theologians. Many of the pastors and church leaders will support an educational and training program to qualify certain ones of their members to become Certified Public Theologians and therapeutic leaders.

7. Practical therapy is consistent with the Holy Scriptures. The inexhaustible knowledge, benevolent teachings and spiritual richness of the Bible contain more than enough righteous instructions, redemptive and salvation resourcefulness to heal and restore the brokenness of humanity and the nations of the world. The knowledge, wisdom, understanding and spiritual guidance are available in abundance for the practice of public theology and practical therapeutic healings for the wounded, broken hearted, neglected, rejected and victimized.

The above-enumerated premises are for the most part, true, reasonable and acceptable. They are consistent with the theme of practicality and the objectives and goals of public theology and practical therapy. Practical therapy is used in conjunction with public theology because practical therapy has a theological perspective within the context of its use in this work. Theology is that indispensable connection with the knowledge and Will of

God in all human affairs. Practical therapy is inclusive of common sense, sound judgment, professionalism, ethics and morality. Biblical authority and theological guidance are essential in the practice of practical therapy.

The essentials of the practice of practical therapy will be presented in a separate publication.

CHAPTER 13

The Practice of Public Theology

The Spiritual Domain

The optimum effective practice of public theology requires the incorporation of the spiritual domain of human knowledge and discernment as an integral primary value of human life. The spiritual domain acknowledges the passion and compassion of the heart and the capacity of the soul for love of self, others and God. The spiritual domain encompasses these entities and qualities that make human communion, compassion and union possible and significant.

It is through the spiritual domain that enables human beings to relate to God through faith. It is through the spiritual domain that humans are able to transcend the here and now, the physical and tangible, and that which is seen and heard. It operates beyond the cognitive, affective and conative domains (psychomotor).

The Holy Bible confirms and validates the spiritual domain. It is a body of the most significant knowledge known to mankind. It has influenced civilization more than any other knowledge known to mankind. It has endured for thousands of years and still maintains a current and future relevance. The Bible is replete with instances where men and women with insufficient facts, took actions based on faith, love and hope against overwhelming opposition and insurmountable odds. The Book of Hebrews, the eleventh chapter, gives a long list of biblical heroes who accomplished astounding and miraculous successes by FAITH. They did the incredible and the impossible through the spiritual domain of faith. The historical validity of the spiritual domain has already been established and authorized as abiding truth revealed by God. The Apostle Paul highlights the fruit of the Spirit as, "love, joy, peace, longsuffering, gentleness, goodness, faith, meekness, temperance; against such there is no law." (Galatians 5:22 – 23 KJV)

There are many requirements and responsibilities of the spiritual domain. These requirements and responsibilities are found in the Bible from Genesis to Revelation. These requirements are the basic tenets for public theological operation. When a people adhere to these spiritual requirements, they find peace, prosperity and salvation. Therefore, it is important to enumerate some of the required traits and values of the spiritual domain. The requirements are to: (1) love (2) repent (3) forgive (4) enlighten (5) strengthen (6) witness the truth (7) be faithful (8) be watchful (9) believe in the truth (10) pray (11) warn (12) feed (13) heal (14) liberate (15) have dominion (16) lead (17) serve (18) rise and shine (19) rebirth (20) convert (21) transform (22) redeem (23) walk humbly (24) do justly.

In addition to those duties to _do_, there are requirements of _being_. The spiritual domain requires us to _be_: (1) loving (2) joyful (3) peaceful (4) longsuffering (5) gentle (6) temperate (7) faithful (8) courageous (9) humble (10) compassionate (11) wise and understanding (12) just and merciful.

It must be understood that the above spiritual traits and values do not lend themselves to the objectivity of test tube analysis or other scientific laboratory investigation and observation. Nevertheless, these traits and values are real. They have real consequences and impact in the lives of people and society. True science and true spirituality do not conflict with each other. Although they may be different kinds of reality, they are complementary in the pursuit of social progress and human salvation. It is well known by scholars and acknowledged by scientists, that scientific explanations do not exhaust the meaning of things. People were using the spiritual and religious domains of knowledge long before the advent of scientific knowledge and methods began in history.

It is most unfortunate that somewhere along the way, the American public educational system divorced itself from the formal teaching of the Bible and Christianity in its schools. The subsequent spiritual/Christian knowledge deficit has significantly imperiled the spiritual and ethical health of the nation and the world. It is unwise, irresponsible and dangerous to educate minds and ignore the ethical, moral and spiritual guidance of those minds. Human beings possess moral and spiritual capacities. Our educational systems have allowed these spiritual and moral capacities to exist as vacuums. Since, "nature abhors a vacuum," these neglected and empty capacities are being filled with alien moralities and evil spirits.

It is the challenge of public theologians to seize upon this opportunity at this late time in history to specialize and major in the spiritual domain in transmitting the highest ethical, moral and spiritual knowledge known to mankind. It is the incomparable revelatory good news knowledge of the Holy Bible, which culminated in the salvation knowledge of Jesus Christ. This is the knowledge that must fill the vacuums of the heart, soul and spirits of this misguided, confused and lost generation.

There are some hopeful signs to turn the rushing tides of human self-destruction. One sign is the passage of legislation in the State of Georgia in 2006, that allows for the teaching of the Bible in the public high schools of Georgia. This law does not require the student to take the Bible course, but it is available as an elective subject or course. Even with the restrictions placed upon the teaching of the Bible, it is a hopeful sign that ethical, moral, spiritual and salvation knowledge is beginning to be made available to students who attend public high schools in Georgia. Another hopeful sign is that mankind is learning everyday that the dramatic increase in secular and scientific technology has, ironically, made the world an unprecedented more dangerous place. Civilization is now living on the brink of cataclysmic disaster. Under these circumstances, even secular-minded, thoughtful men, must now come to the realization that the hope in secularistic salvation is futile. In mankind's desperate search for peace and survival, he is forced to look to God and God's long ignored plan of salvation in Jesus Christ. All other tried remedies and solutions have been exhausted without success.

The spiritual domain is a mandatory must option as the way out of darkness. The challenge for world peace and world survival and salvation is a theological challenge. Those persons who proclaim to know the will, ways, works and wisdom of God, must now arise to the challenge to point the way for humanity. The challenge is to add the transforming spiritual dimension to our secularistic, pluralistic, diverse and decaying culture. The practice of public theology is ready to implement this plan with the spiritual domain.

It is important that the public theologians lead the way in assuring the American society and the institutions of government that it is lawful and that it is okay to add the spiritual domain to the American democratic public life, and the public education system. This simply means that spirituality and religion in public life will no longer be ignored and denied. This inherent tradition and foundation of American freedom and democracy must be acknowledged and embraced as a blessing from God. God has blessed America. God has shed his grace on America.

America was established under God with allegiance and trust in God. Our currency, Declaration of Independence, Pledge of Allegiance, oath of office and patriotic songs fully acknowledge God in our national life. The "Negro National Anthem" concludes by saying, "May we forever stand. True to our God, true to our native land."

The spiritual domain was most emphatically expressed in America during the 17th, 18th, and 19th centuries. These powerful religious forces were known as the great awakening. The great awakening in America was characterized by a long list of highly motivated and inspired preachers of the Gospel. There were great movements of evangelicalism and revivalism. It was a spiritual movement to evangelize America and the world. This spiritual movement brought about massive conversions. It was an extraordinary outpouring of God's saving grace in Jesus Christ. A broad set of campaigns were put in motion to reform America as a result of this great awakening. This great spiritual awakening influenced all aspects of American life. It was led by ministers of the Christian Gospel. American democracy was born out of this culture of Christianity. Democracy in America has been created, nurtured and sustained by Christianity. Therefore, it is ludicrous for the government or any other entity to deny or disavow the spiritual domain. The spiritual domain supersedes, under girds and supports the other domains. The spiritual domain is the bonafide parent of the other domains. Human wholeness cannot be achieved without the appropriate integration of the thinking of the mind, feelings or the emotions, actions of the body and being of the spirit.

It is the important role of public theology to bring together the sacred and secular aspects of society in a positive and peaceful way for the common good of humanity. Democracy offers an opportunity for a mutual cooperation between the sacred and the secular. Both are under the jurisdiction of God. It is the role of public theology to create a positive alliance between church and state, democracy and religion, the human and the divine. The righteous rule of government is not to dominate religion or society; but rather, to assure social justice, freedom and equality for all the people.

Christian theology speaks to all faiths and all people. The Christian role is not to dominate government or the people but to transform them and to redeem them through the mercy and righteousness of God and the sacrificial love and grace of Jesus Christ. The public theologian seeks to provide the leadership and directions to overcome the barriers and confusion that separate and alienate humanity.

There is much work to be done by the public theologian as the spiritual domain is integrated with the other domains. In all the agencies and institutions of society the spiritual domain must be considered. How must the spiritual domain be incorporated in the government employment and the employment process and procedures? What information must be placed on employment applications and other registration forms to include the spiritual or faith identification of the applicants and registrants? How must the spiritual and faith aspects of the clients be incorporated in hospitals and other healthcare facilities? How must spiritual assessments, evaluations, planning and treatment goals be approached and instituted in the healthcare facilities?

The questions above must be answered with extensive general and contextualized education and training in public theology and the spiritual domain.

In the process and efforts to learn who a person really is, it has become critical to learn their spiritual identification. It is no longer sufficient to adequately identify a person by the traditional personal data of race, sex, age, place of birth and educational levels and a photograph of the person. It is now mandatory that we know something about a person's spirit in order to know the person. We need to know something about their personal and intimate belief systems and value systems. We need to know whether they believe in the only God with a capital G. We need to know if their religion is valid. We need to know if their creeds are true. We need to know if their doctrines are sound. We need to know whether they serve God or idol gods. We need to know whether a person lives in and relates to a world of sobriety and reality within a historical context; or whether it is a mystical world of illusions, fantasies and fiction. Ultimately, we need to know if a person identifies with the Spirit of God or a spirit not of God. (1 John 4:1-2 KJV) The establishment of a spiritual identification is most significant and in some cases, critical. A person's primary identification is related to their ultimate beliefs and commitments.

Curriculum for Public Theology

An educational curriculum for public theology must be designed to equip the public theologian to effectively meet the culture crisis leadership challenge in the twenty first century. Public theologians must make critical decisions. Decisions with such magnitude must be based on an extraordinary resource of specialized knowledge. In addition to being leaders for humanity, the public theologians must be teachers of humanity. They must have the prophetic insight and proclaim a prophetic voice. They must be watchmen on the wall looking out from the high towers for the safety and welfare of humanity. Physical lookout walls and physical high towers are obsolete in the twenty-first century. Therefore, the curriculum must include a new way of watching out for the welfare of humanity. The enemy is not necessarily another race, culture, nation or religion. The enemy to humanity may very well be among your own and cloaked in various disguises of deception. Therefore, the public theologian must be able to discern and test spirits to determine whether they are of God. The public theologian must be the eyes, ears, hands, head and heart of God. The public theology curriculum must be established with these faculties in mind.

The effective practice of public theology requires substantial knowledge and understanding of the Holy Bible and the saving grace in Jesus Christ. Additionally, some core knowledge in the enumerated areas below is also essential for the education of the public theologian:

1. <u>Divine, natural and statutory laws.</u>
   The resolution of conflicting laws to rule humanity with valid and legitimate authority.

2. <u>Political science.</u>
   Who has the right to govern and by what authority? How is that right obtained and executed?

3. <u>Economic consumption.</u>
   What methodology assures the fair and equitable distribution or allocation of the resources of God?

4. <u>Religious pluralism.</u>
   How can religion be validated as true? What is a valid religion?

5. <u>Global business accounting.</u>
   Who controls the means of production? How should God's resources be allocated? What jobs and businesses are needed based on human priorities and needs?

6. <u>Global geography.</u>
   How can the standards and quality of life be balanced globally?

7. <u>Human heterogeneity.</u>
   How can human differences be translated and transformed into positive complementary attributes? How can they be blended into one harmonious human family?

8. <u>Ethnicities and sectarianism.</u>
   How can group prejudices and conflicts be overcome peacefully? How can the narrow local loyalties be universalized into one loyalty under God?

9. <u>Morality and ethics.</u>
   How can true universal moral and ethical standards be established based on validated truth?

10. <u>Patriotism, national and global.</u>
    How can universal loyalties be inclusive of national patriotism? How can immigrants be American patriots when they have transplanted the patriotism of their own native lands? How can the conflicting loyalties be resolved?

11. <u>Autonomous technology.</u>
    How can public theology provide proactive guidance to scientific technology?

12. <u>Environmental stewardship.</u>
    Who must be responsible for the leadership and decision-making for the custodial care and the guardianship of the global natural environment?

Based on the above questions and issues, a public theological curriculum can be developed. This is not an exhaustive curriculum. However, the core knowledge is covered.

The curriculum must be broad and adequate. It does not have to be exhaustive and all-inclusive because one of the responsibilities of the public theologian is to develop alliances with other disciplines and areas of knowledge. However, I believe that the curriculum challenge is clear. In order for the public theologian to be effective and meet the extraordinary challenges of humanity, a broader, more specialized and contextualized educational curriculum must be employed.

Commitments to the Practice

The effective practice of public theology will require the following commitments:

1. <u>Be faithful to God</u>, who intervened in recent history to rescue and bring a helpless and downtrodden people through the wilderness of slavery and degradation and used them in the great awakening and transforming of America into a land of freedom and opportunity.

2. <u>Be loyal to the faith in Jesus Christ</u>, who is a unique gift of God with eternal life, hope, healing, restoration, liberation and salvation. He declares never to leave us or forsake those who believe in him. He was uniquely resurrected in history.

3. <u>Hold on to the survival values</u> from Genesis to Revelation; the legacies and heritage of the forefathers. Diligently prepare your children and the oncoming generation with intellectual competence and the courage to maintain their birthrights and leave posterity for the succeeding generations.

4. <u>Be diligent in seeking truth</u>, knowledge, wisdom and understanding to lift your people and mankind to greater heights of human civility and spiritual redemption.

5. <u>Resolve to commit to and invest in the maximum development of your people</u>, beginning from the cradle. Spare no expense in providing the best education possible for their health, heads, hearts and hands to glorify God.

6. <u>Be resolute in equipping yourself and your people</u> for escalated spiritual warfare, cultural conflicts, economic deprivation, political corruption, social injustice, environmental pollution, religious confusion, technological dangers, turmoil and terroristic warfare.

7. <u>Select and develop pastors and leaders who are biblically grounded</u>, theologically guided, spiritually enriched, compassionately committed and courageously empowered to teach, preach and practice the liberating and transforming Gospel of Jesus Christ in a world in conflict and crisis and to a rebellious and perverse generation.

8. <u>Institutionalize the sound doctrines and the core values</u> of survival and triumph, and transmit them to your people; in families, schools, churches and other institutions in the society. Institutionalize skills for living, ethical principles, professional standards, the histories and legacies of human successes inspired by God.

9. <u>Create environments conducive to the optimum development, growth and achievement</u> for the human potential and the human spirit. Create educational environments where students can learn to the maximum of their potential. Create home environments where God's purpose for fathers, mothers, sons and daughters and families can be fulfilled.

10. <u>Create a community through public theology</u> where there is understanding, cooperation and concern among the neighbors and a habitation of safety, cleanliness and beauty. Create an atmosphere in government where there is commitment to social

justice, equal opportunities, and equitable distribution of goods and services. Create a government environment where there will be pro-activities for peace, social justice, freedom and prosperity.

11. <u>Create workplace environments through public theology</u> where respect, fairness, cooperation and teamwork prevail. Such a workplace recognizes the human dignity of every employee and every person. The workplace ought to be a place where each worker can carry out his or her assignment without conflict and confusion and where there is harmony and a healthy environment where persons strive with goodwill to reach common goals.

12. <u>Create church environments and organizations</u> where the expressions of God in word, in music, in prayer, in praise, in worship, in adoration, in service and practice will be an overflowing of love and truth that lifts, inspires, enlightens, unifies, redeems and transforms. Create a church environment that inspires, trains, educates, and prepares men and women to be skilled practitioners of public theology.

Willie James Webb

The Practice of Public Theology

Human Protective Standards

It is the duty and the challenge of public theology to establish standards and models during the course of human commerce and interactions that will protect human beings and their God-given rights and values. This is no simple task because individual rights and interests must be balanced with the rights and interests of the common good, as well as the corporate interest of all people. Due to the ongoing dynamic social processes and changes, human standards and models must be constantly observed, evaluated, assessed and adjusted for ongoing human protection on all levels. Society is not static. It is in constant flux and change.

The 21st century has brought about unprecedented social changes – the mixing and mingling of diverse people, races, cultures, ethnicities, values, beliefs and religions. The limits of accommodation and toleration are making it difficult for the other essential social processes of cooperation, assimilation and integration to be accomplished. The resulting tensions and conflicts have been made more dangerous due to technological advances and the potential of nuclear warfare. It is these set of circumstances that has made it mandatory for universally sound human protective standards. Local standards and narrow loyalties must give way and make way for universal standards set by God with the highest loyalty to the incarnate God of Jesus Christ. One human family in one world must accept the Will, the way, the truth, and the sovereign rule of the one God of the universe. The duty and challenge of the public theologian is to establish standards according to the laws, love, and Will of God.

The book of Hebrews 1:1-2 acknowledges that God has spoken at various times in different manners through the Prophets to the fathers, but in these last days, God has spoken to His people through his Son, Jesus Christ. Jesus Christ is the authority. He is the stability, which underlies the transitory processes of the universe. The Gospel of Jesus Christ and the Mind of Christ through the Holy Spirit is always current and relevant to provide the answers for our constantly changing and complex problems. It is through the spiritual domain and the Mind of Christ that the public theologian uses and consults to provide the true, righteous, and just answers to our escalating culture crisis.

The public theologian takes positions, advocates, establishes policies, and takes action for the establishment of human protective standards. The following enumerations for protective standards are not considered to be exhaustive or complete. They are the beginning for an ongoing development of protective standards for implementation and enhancement by persons who are committed to the cause of human salvations in Christ.

We must be diligent in establishing human protective standards to avoid irreversible deterioration and decay in human society. Standards that put human welfare and human life at risk must be avoided and eliminated. In all areas of human life, the question must be asked: "Does this law, policy, action, construction, or position provide the optimum protection for human life?"

Standards that put human life at risk are unjust. A society can become over-saturated with injustice. Injustice creates deficits in the human potential. The challenges of the 21st century require surpluses and not deficits in the human potential. It is vital that the human potential of every person be actualized to the maximum. The wasted human potential in school dropouts, alcohol and other drug addictions, criminal behavior, unemployment, homelessness, mental illness, wars and wastefulness must cease. We can optimize the human potential by making a deliberate decision to do so and do it en mass.

God is calling on individuals and institutions alike to make things right. God is calling on whoever will heed the call for correcting wrongs, bringing about righteousness and administering justice. Every believer can participate in this endeavor. The public theologian may be the one to make the declaration of righteousness, send out warnings and to sound the alarm. However, it is the duty of all believers and disciplines to get involved in the establishment of human protective standards.

The human protective standards enumerated in this edition is seeking persons with the interest and the expertise to become writers, exponents and advocates of these human protective standards, or of others of their own choosing. We must begin today to stop cooperating with unrighteousness and injustice and begin to get things right in all human affairs.

Positions, Advocacy, Policies and Actions

For The Establishment of Human Protective Standards

1. Publicly displayed sexual activity is harmful to the common good of society and especially to children and youth. Standards must be established to avoid and prevent the public display of explicit sexual activity. The news media must establish responsible policies in this area of programming.

2. Same sex marriage, homosexual activity and sexually linked same sex domestic partnerships are deviations from the established standards of the natural order. The promotion of these practices is harmful, confusing and destructive to the institution of marriage, families and especially the protection of children. Same sex relationships are based on invalid principles and unsound doctrines that cannot be universalized. Same sex marriage and homosexual activity work against the common good of society. This is not intended by any means to be a condemnation of persons with same sex orientation. It is for the

encouragement of healthy lifestyles and for the public good. God loves all His children. He has set standards for all His children. God has set standards for all creation. Divine laws and natural laws are created and authorized by the Creator, God. The fluctuating and sometimes arbitrary statutory laws made by man cannot legitimately and authoritatively usurp the laws made by God. The divine and natural law of God may be denied, opposed and ignored. Nevertheless, they are unmistakably and inherently there/here as abiding realities beyond the power and authority of humankind. We must be careful not to esteem, celebrate or worship sex beyond the purpose and responsibilities of marriage.

3. The public display of licking, kissing and other oral contacts between dogs (as well as other animals) and a human is an unnatural expression of affection and is harmful to the common good of society. Standards must be set to prohibit the elevation of a dog or other animals to a cohabitation level with human beings. This unnatural oral, licking and kissing of dogs and humans must be prohibited by television and other public media showings.

4. It is grossly irresponsible and outrageous that dangerous dogs continue to attack and kill people. Strict standards and strict laws and strict enforcement must be established to protect individuals in all communities from the exposure and attacks of dangerous dogs. The responsible government agencies must be diligent and vigorous in solving this lethal problem and public nuisance.

5. There is a gross lack of protection of the public in the food service industry. The laws, standards and enforcement are woefully inadequate in restaurants

and other public eating establishments. Strangers with unknown health histories and unverified backgrounds can get a job in food services in most food service establishments. This is especially true in Georgia. We are insisting that adequate food service laws and standards be established and enforced that require, as a minimum:

(A) A health certificate based on a physical examination by a licensed Boardcertified physician;

(B) Sanitary training for food service workers;

(C) Appropriate hygiene and sanitized uniforms by food service workers, and

(D) Regular, random inspections of all areas of food storage, preparation, utensils, equipment and service areas.

6. Customers for barber, beauty and other body care salons must be assured, with appropriate notices and publications, that the facilities have acceptable standards of cleanliness, sanitation, safety and certified training and professionalism. The certifying and licensing agencies must assure that customers are protected. The burden of protection must **not** be placed on the customers.

7. Healthcare facilities at every level must develop safety standards that will provide the highest protective level possible to protect their patients from safety and health hazards while in the care of the health providers. Negligence, health hazards and medical mistakes are at exceptionally unacceptable high levels. It is recommended that the appropriate corrections

8. Greed, malpractice, fraud, theft, deceptions and unprofessionalism are rampant in too many businesses. It is strongly recommended that business ethics education and training be required for all persons who work in the business public sector. Adequate and acceptable ethical practices in all businesses serving the public are recommended.

9. How can consumers of the automobile repair industry be protected from deceptive and fraudulent practices? Policies and procedures must be developed to protect customers from fraudulent and unscrupulous practices in the automobile repair industry.

10. It is recommended that the selection of music played in restaurants and other leisure and recreational areas be conducive to relaxation, conversation, reflection, peace and tranquility. Loud, rhythmic, noisy and emotionally stimulating music works against enjoyment, dialogue, peace and reflection. It is recommended that the selection of music in public restaurants and similar facilities consider the customers need for peace, quietness, relaxation, conversation, refinement and family values, as well as cultural and spiritual values. Loud rhythmic noises contribute to abuse and violence.

11. It is recommended that legislation be passed that requires, with specificity, appropriate and sufficient road signs and signals that provides clear and timely directions for motorists to make driving decisions without confusion and jeopardy to highway and road safety.

be made and the appropriate inspections, monitoring and accountability be instituted.

12. There is a significant problem in seeing and locating addresses from roadways and streets in most of our municipalities. It can be frustrating, stressful, time-consuming and a road safety hazard. It is recommended that legislation be passed to require the readable visibility of street numbers of all addresses on all buildings form the street. Unclear addresses are distracting to drivers and pose traffic hazards.

13. The disciplinary problems in our Public School Systems are very detrimental to the educational process and it contributes significantly to our social ills. The school disciplinary problem is fixable. CAPT is appealing to the school superintendents, the Boards and principals to institute immediately the necessary policies, remedies and procedures to fix the disciplinary problems in the Public School Systems. Representatives of CAPT are available to make recommendations toward that end.

14. There is a lack of uniformity and seriousness in the presentations of programs in the school during Black History Month in February. CAPT is appealing to the educational systems to develop a more meaningful, relevant, redeeming, and universally applicable Black History curriculum to be presented in all of the public schools in the month of February. Black History in America has invaluable messages for the world and for all people. CAPT representatives are available to provide assistance in this regard.

15. The state of Georgia, during the 2006 legislative session, passed legislation that allows for the literary and historical teaching of the Bible in the Public School Systems of Georgia. The legislation is said to be permissive and not mandatory. However, CAPT is recommending that each educational entity of the

applicable schools in Georgia adopt the curriculum or otherwise make the elective Bible course available to every student who chooses to take the Bible course. Inasmuch as the state has approved the Bible course, it is now the right of every student in Georgia Public Schools to have the Bible course made available to them.

16. A well-planned assembly program in the school system can be very helpful in instilling values, building character, positive self-esteem and identity, motivation for achievement, and the promotion of excellence, scholarship, leadership and service. CAPT is recommending to the respective school Boards, superintendents and principals of Georgia Public Schools, K-12, to institute weekly, a well-designed weekly assembly program for all students. A weekly assembly program has significant potential in building a strong, positive school spirit and school pride. An inspirational singing of the school song weekly would reinforce positive attitudes and a spirit of unity.

17. Computerized online technology is effectively eliminating millions of Americans from participating and accessing in the process of getting goods and services of which they are entitled. The elimination of the traditional means and ways of accessing entitled goods and services is happening unchecked at a rapid rate. This technological deprivation and/or inaccessibility are causing serious civil rights violations.

The necessity and requirement of computerized technology to access the means of goods and services effectively discriminates against a large and growing class of American citizens. This technological discrimination deprives those persons who do not have computers or accessibility to computer technology of an equal opportunity for accessing and utilizing the availability of goods and services.

Laws must be instituted and enforced to protect and insure that the entitlement to access and utilize available public services for those citizens who do not have access to computer technology. Computer technology is imposing an unnatural disadvantage to citizens and persons who do not have the respective technological capability. It is an imposed deprivation not necessarily due to any fault of the technologically deprived. Laws have been instituted to accommodate the physically and mentally challenged. Therefore, it is only logical, fair and reasonable to institute technological accommodation laws to insure equality of opportunity for the technologically disadvantaged. To avoid complete dependence on computer technology, it is also recommended that adequate traditional means of accessing and utilizing public services be maintained. Computer technology is not absolute. It depends on electrical power, which goes out from time to time.

18. The reformation of the Criminal Justice System has great potential for education, training, rehabilitation, reducing crime, building character, and more responsible and productive citizens. This can be done by educating and training this captive population. It can be done by providing mental health, alcohol and drug treatment services in all detention and correctional institutions. It can be done through Bible study and worship. CAPT is recommending that funding and professional education, treatment and pastoral staff be established in the criminal justice detention and correctional facilities. It is

recommended that the churches provide ongoing pastoral ministry for the Criminal Justice System.

19. Judges and lawyers arbitrate and litigate and make decisions regarding the most precious values and sacred rights of human beings. This includes life, liberty, property, the quality of living, and the allocation of resources. Judges and lawyers are trained primarily in statutory law. Most judicial decisions are based on statutory law. Natural law and Divine law provided by God are routinely excluded from judicial decision-making in the American judicial system.

In order for lawyers, judges, and others who arbitrate the rights of individuals to be more accurate and comprehensive in their deliberations, mediations and decisions, it is recommended that appropriate theological courses be added to the legal law curriculum. Law schools and theological seminaries must become allies in the training of lawyers and judges. How can a judge legitimately decide the case involving "Creationism vs. Evolutionary Theory" without valid theological knowledge?

20. In view of the hazards of crime, fires, floods and other natural disasters, building codes must be reviewed and modified to build safe and substantial homes and other structures to protect human life and property. The building industry must be monitored by the appropriate authority to insure that life, property and human rights and health are protected from hazardous, defective, and otherwise faulty materials, structures and environments. Building codes must be written and enforced to provide the optimum protection and security for human life, property, rights of individuals and for the common good.

21. Churches must take the lead in advocating and providing for love, protection, care and the Christian education and training of children. Churches must get involved in parenting education and the early mentoring of children and youth. Parents must be taught to take greater responsibility for building character and instilling healthy values in their children, and more involvement with the respective schools and the parent/teacher association is a necessity.

22. The elderly population is increasing at a rapid rate. Increasingly, the quality of living declines for the elderly due to the need for more healthcare and services as they get older. Many of these seniors end up in nursing homes among strangers and sometimes with uncaring workers in substandard living conditions. The church must lead the way in providing the optimum level of care and compassion for our senior citizens. This will require commitment, training and resources. We must not be cheap or negligent with those persons who paved the way for us.

23. Public theology is encouraging technology to use its creativity and innovation to design equipment, instruments, materials, electronics, and devices to enhance the efficiency and independence of the elderly and disabled.

24. The Christian Association of Public Theologians (CAPT) is appealing to all colleges and universities to include in your educational curriculum, courses in public theology. It is unintelligent and irrational to ignore and exclude the Biblical knowledge of God and Jesus Christ from a liberal and free educational system. The hope of human survival and salvation

are found in Biblical Christian theology. It is the duty and the responsibility of higher education to make available the knowledge that has influenced western civilization and the world more than any other knowledge. This knowledge is contained in the Holy Bible. We must recognize and add ethics to the other three domains of learning.

Secular public education is primarily limited to the following domains of learning: (A) Cognitive, (B) Affective, and (C) Psycho-motor.

The Cognitive includes the intellect and the mind. The Affective includes emotions and feelings. The Psycho-motor relates to bodily activity and behavior. The excluded learning domain is the spiritual domain. The spiritual domain is about the soul, ethics, morality, and religion. It is about the human relationship to the Creator that is contained in the Holy Bible and other expressions. CAPT advocates the inclusion of the spiritual theological domain to be included in the public educational systems.

25. Noah did not wait for the flood to come before he made preparations to save a remnant of humanity. Noah built an ark with gopher wood and homemade crude instruments. In spite of the wickedness and corruption of the people of the earth, Noah found grace in the eyes of God. Moreover, God gave Noah instructions on how to survive the Great Flood.

Global warming, tsunamis, earthquakes, and other natural disasters are threats to humanity on the earth. God's grace and mercy are available. He promises his people who are called by His name that He will heal the land if they "humble themselves, pray, seek His face and turn from their wicked ways." (2Chronicles

7:14) God has blessed mankind with the knowledge, technology and resources to live on the water, under the water, and the capability to fly above it.

God has warned humanity of the looming dangers to the people on the earth. Why can't the people of the world and the nations of the earth recognize the common threat to **all** humanity; stop the wars and the squandering of resources, turn to God and embrace a survival strategy for humanity? We **must** do more than talk about dangers and go on with business as usual. God has shown us the dangers. It is now time to respond with the highest ethical, spiritual and theological guidance, and the full arsenal of scientific and technological resources. Human life was the ultimate concern of Jesus Christ. It **must** be our concern as well!

26. It is urgent that public theologians get involved in the spiritual and ideological raging warfare. It is these evil ideological spirits that are the driving forces behind greed, injustice, jealousy, arrogance, crime, violence and wars. Military might is not sufficient to destroy the various expressions and disguises of spiritual wickedness and spiritual darkness. The theologians must make preparations; devise strategies and methods to get involved in the ideological warfare. God has shown us and demonstrated in nature and in history and in His Word that which is good, true, righteous, just, merciful, compassionate, Holy and loving. The Bible is overflowing with the inexhaustible riches of God and His Christ. The message must get out of "the Book," outside the church walls, and into the public square and marketplaces of the world.

27. Re-evaluate privatization and policies. A number of questions must be asked about privatization, which includes the following:

(A) Was the establishment of privatization done legally and constitutionally?

(B) Is privatization based on a sound doctrine and established democratic principles?

(C) Were the citizens, voters and general public provided an opportunity to be informed, discuss, approve, and cast votes for privatization?

(D) What are the criteria and guidelines for determining what can and cannot be privatized and the qualifications and requirements for privatization contracts?

(E) Who and what office in the State of Georgia administers privatization and where is the location of the operation (s)? (This applies to other relevant states as well.)

(F) Please provide the information necessary for the citizens and the public to communicate with the Office of Privatization. This is a request for the name of the director, the address of the privatization office, telephone, e-mail and Web site.

28. Effective legislation and policies are requested to protect citizens and the public from identity theft. This legislation must include appropriate safeguards, requirements by institutions, and agencies that require the provision of personal information, such as birth date, Social Security Number, and Drivers' License as a prerequisite to their service. The legislation must

require personal and technological safeguards against the transmission, access, and disposal of public personal information that can be used for theft of identity. It is noted that the picture identification, along with the accompanying information on drivers' licenses in the State of Georgia, can be retrieved and reproduced by the State Patrol personnel. What policy and procedure is there to safeguard against the retrieval of this personal information by the Georgia State Patrol for unauthorized purposes?

29. The leaders of the international governments and the international leaders representing the one true God of the universe must convene and establish acceptable civilized standards of conduct for all human beings. Those standards must include:

(A) The respect, reverence, and sacredness of all human life.

(B) The inherent right to be free of human bondage and involuntary servitude.

(C) The right to be free from the malice, harm and violation of other human beings, physically, mentally, spiritually, and socially.

Those uncivilized behaviors must be condemned and eliminated that harm human life and violate human rights. The international community must condemn the taking of human life and the violation of human rights. The international community must condemn and eliminate the violations, the violence, and the taking of innocent human lives, as well as the social and cultural breeding grounds for such ungodly violations.

30. The government and the church must take the leadership to establish equitable merit systems for equality of opportunities and services. Arbitrary, capricious, discriminatory assignments of goods and services create unjust and harmful social and political systems in the society. Social justice is a prerequisite to the higher values in society. Ethical merit systems are vital for social balance.

31. The bureaucratic automated electronic answering systems are very damaging, as well as costly and inefficient for consumers. It is not unusual to wait for 30 minutes, or more, to contact a human being for simple services. In many instances, these automated services are inefficient, time-consuming, and stressful. This automated system **must** be evaluated and changed for the benefit and welfare of consumers and citizens.

Summary

The practice of public theology seeks to make known the ways and means of implementing God's blueprint for human survival. The public theologian is charged with designing systems and methods to make the agencies and institutions in society to function more effectively and benevolently for the public good. Public theology has this capability through its understanding of biblical knowledge and revelation from God. Public theology recognizes, embraces and espouses the supreme standards for living set by God in the Holy Bible and the life and teachings of Jesus Christ. Public theology is not a dictatorial form of government. It is an enlightening and righteous way of living, believing and sharing according to the standards set by God for the common good of all people. Public theology has that capability to design systems to accomplish those standards of living.

The practice of public theology includes the designing, as well as the operation of community agencies and institutions. This is not to say that theology has not already played a major role in designing and operating community agencies and institutions. The emphasis here is that public theology must become more proactive and make it a top priority in the designing and operating community agencies and institutions.

Since there is no off limits to the jurisdiction of God, the public theologian has an authorized and legitimate role to play in all community agencies and institutions. There are many institutions in the society that are in need of more effective functionality. Generally speaking, they are religious institutions, educational, family, government, industrial, health, criminal justice, media, sports and recreation, science and technology, international relations and the institution of world religions. It must be noted that the theological design of these agencies and institutions Is not to make them religious, but to make them function more efficiently and effectively for the common good. Public theology includes scientific, artistic and all forms of valid and true knowledge to accomplish the goal.

The role of the public theologian in the practice of public theology is not an attempt to know all, be all, or do all. The role of the public theologian is a catalyst to enhance, clarify and make more effective the roles of others. The results of the impact of public theology will be done by many persons and professions who are not public theologians. However, they are very effective, purpose driven, courageous and noble in what they do. They are effective because they apply their Christian faith to what they do. They apply their faith to their profession. The ultimate objectives and goals of the practice of public theology is that it will translate into the practice of Christian living in all walks of life.

I have been so gratified and so pleased to find persons who apply their Christian faith to their profession. I have encountered Christian doctors, school teachers, secretaries, counselors, college professors, cooks, bus drivers, custodians, mechanics, administrators, public officials, IRS workers, police offers and many others. I am convinced that there are many persons in the world of work and in corporate and government bureaucracies who are committed believers in Jesus Christ. Many of these persons do not wear Christian titles, carry Bibles or do religious talk. However, many are providing helpful and compassionate Christian services. Their light is shining and they are radiating the goodness of God as they serve, sometimes quietly, their clients, their company and their people. These persons may not have the credentials to qualify them as public theologians, but they are disciples when they follow Christ. In the sense of providing human compassionate services, it is an expression of public theology.

The practice of public theology encourages open Christianity and public discipleship. This simply means that you make known to all people by your living and professing that you are a believer and a follower of Jesus Christ. There are many public disciples who work in the secular world. There are many ministers and pastors who work in the secular world. The practice of public theology encourages Christians to work inside, as well as outside of the so called, "system." No special credentials are needed to be a follower of Christ. Therefore, all believers can qualify for discipleship.

There are many Christian disciples who work in the secular world. There are great challenges to the Christian disciples in the secular world. There are at the same time great opportunities for transformation, salvation and redemption in the secular world. Public theology is calling all Christian disciples, where ever they may be, to begin to practice their faith in appropriate and effective ways. The spiritual domain of the Holy Spirit is a coworker in building this kingdom on earth and establishing human protective standards for the precious and sacred gift of life. Become intentional and constantly mindful of your responsibility as a disciple, minister, believer, theologian, and a child of God, to practice your faith through good works, goodwill, love and hope.

CHAPTER 14

Theological Responsibility for Public Policy

The purpose of a public policy is to provide some built in authoritative assurance for the direction and guidance of correlated public actions. It is an influential tool of deliberate planning to assure more probable and predictable outcomes of human behaviors and social actions.

A public policy can be designed to protect and enhance human life and human values and assure compliance with applicable laws, ethical codes, corporate goals and the mission of the respective organizational entity. A public policy can assist in creating a healthy social environment, uphold and respect human dignity and the human rights of all people.

Since public policy can have such a broad impact on people and society, it is only logical and natural that theology must be a part of that process in formulating public policy. The advocacy for the inclusion of the theological perspective in the making of public policy is not intended to monopolize or to exclude other relevant perspectives. The intention is to include the theological perspective as a vital component which has been left out in most instances for many decades. The addition of the theological perspective in public policy and decision making can be vital in the critical times of the 21st century.

True public theology does not seek to dominate the public policy making process within the framework of a democratic form of government. Public theology is broad enough and inclusive enough to accept relevant truths from other perspectives. True public theology must be a foremost guardian of freedom and democracy and must guard against fanaticism, sectarianism, cultism and dogmatic short sightedness. The goal in the public policy making process is to be receptive to a healthy inclusion and an equitable balance that reflects representative participation.

Translating Theology into Public Policy

The public theologian may work on the inside or outside of the venues of public policy making. There are an infinite number of ways to influence public policy by the public theologian. These ways of influencing public policy do not have to be dramatic, extreme or radical in order to be effective. There is too much energy and too many resources being used to condemn America and America's institutions for being misguided and lost. It would be more useful and productive to help America and her institutions to rise up from bad policies, failures, misguidance and lostness. We must forgive America for her past sins and mistakes. We must also ask God to forgive us for our negligence, trespasses and sins.

When we have had a sober reflection regarding our individual joint and corporate mistakes and sins; we can cast away the lethal self destructive baggage of the past, and go forward with new plans, policies and renewed hope. Let us put away the blame and the shame and seize this opportunity to restore the sacred honor to our name. Much has been given to America. Much is expected of America. It is the sacred responsibility of every American to help America save itself from itself. This can be done when we turn to each other and not against each other. It is hoped that the theological influence will not be limited to the making of public policy, but also to influence public caring and public and national compassion and a genuine patriotism.

It must be remembered and reiterated again and again that Christian theological influence laid the foundation for the American republic. The Great Awakening in America characterized by massive Christian evangelism, revivals, conversions and expansion in the early 17th century predated the Declaration of Independence of July 4, 1776. It was the Christian influence and Christian values that made possible democracy and the subsequent union of 50 states that constitute the United States of America. Christian values have been the undergirding glue that has held the United States together. There is more truth than is commonly realized when we say and when we sing, "God Bless America." American history suggests very strongly that God has blessed America in special and unique ways, in spite of slavery and the Civil War.

Therefore, the advocacy for theological inclusion in public policy making in America is not new. The precedents for theology involvement in public policy were set in a most dramatic way in the 17th century. This vital sacred legacy of Christian values in the public policies of America must be embraced and preserved. It is the foundational heritage of America. To the extent that Christian values are excluded from public policy, to that same extent America will lose the blessings of God. The cost of such loss is too staggering to contemplate.

Public Policy Initiatives

1. The theologians, including pastors and ministers, must learn how to conduct public policy needs assessments and write credible theological based public policies to be shared with the appropriate persons who make official public policies.

2. The public theologians must be proactive in the formulation of ideas for public policies and having those ideas publicized in the news media to influence the public opinion regarding important public issues.

3. The public theologians must be intentional and deliberate in setting up regular public policy forums in various designated churches or in other community facilities. In order for the meetings to be effective and productive, they must have concrete and practical goals to arrive at specific public policy assessments and specific policy formulations.

4. Public theologians must seek out relevant political and social forums where public policy issues are being discussed and formulated.

5. Public theologians or designees must attend neighborhood association meetings, municipal town hall meetings, NPU (Neighborhood Planning Unit) meetings and other public and community meetings. These various meetings provide an opportunity for the public theologian to learn about public policy information and also to share information regarding public issues and public policies.

6. Public theologians must attend meetings and where possible set specific conferences with respective U. S. senator, congressional representative, state legislator, county commissioner, mayor and city council, educational and other boards and public officials. It is very important to get on their mailing lists and get updates on pending legislation, laws, policies and what is being planned. In most instances constituents are grossly uninformed about public decisions, planning and policies.

7. Invite respective public officials to report and speak on relevant issues to churches and other planned gatherings. Form alliances and coalitions with religions, political, educational and other

social organizations to mobilize meaningful public policies.

8. Pastors must maximize their own church potential and resources for the development of public policy. Many churches have significant numbers of ministers, educators, professional practitioners and public officials.

The above enumerations indicate some practical ways in which theological perspectives can be translated into public policy. Many pastors and ministers of the Gospel preach from their pulpits many sound doctrines that can be translated in molding public opinion and public policy.

The public officials and public policy makers must be challenged to do a better job in keeping their constituents and community informed. It is most tragic for the community to be left out of the public policy making and legislative enactments. It is even more tragic to not be informed or aware of public policies and laws that have been passed and in effect.

Historical Precedents for Public Policy

It is interesting and fascinating that the further we go back in history and beyond history the more we encounter the theological perspective and the spiritual domain. It is the theological perspective that explains and describes the beginning of things. The scriptures that support the historical precedent for public theology are too voluminous to mention. Therefore, only a few scriptures will be used to validate the theological perspectives before the historical advent of other perspectives used in making public policy:

Jeremiah describes in a universal and global way the problems of the earth:

> The earth also is defiled under the inhabitants thereof: Because they have transgressed the laws, changed the ordinance, broken the everlasting covenant. (Jeremiah 24:5 KJV)

Although Jeremiah prophesied in the sixth century B.C. (626-580), two thousand six hundred years ago, he addresses the earth as being defiled in contrast to a nation or some other local place on the earth. He states that this defilement or corruption has come about because the people had transgressed the laws, changed the ordinance and broken the everlasting covenant. Jeremiah's statement implies that God had already instituted public policy and that it is related to an everlasting agreement. When God addresses the whole earth, that has to be public.

Who owns the earth?

Psalm 24 declares that God is the creator and the owner of the earth and the fullness of the earth, the world and they that dwell therein. (Psalm 24, KJV)

Who else can we ascribe as owner of the earth, if not God? Since God is the owner of the earth, the world and everything in it; common sense and simple logic dictate that theology must be involved in the laws, ordinances and covenants that govern the earth. Public policies made on the basis of secularistic detachment from God are misguided and dangerous policies. God created the earth and the inhabitants of the earth. God has also given explicit laws and directions on his will for stewardship and governance of the earth. The Holy Bible is the authoritative source book for human living, actions and interactions.

God speaks inclusively to all people:

> O Earth, Earth, Earth, hear the word of the Lord. (Jeremiah 22:29)

> Hear O Heavens, and give ear, O, Earth; for the Lord hath spoken. (Isaiah 1:2)

The universality of God's message rings out clearly in the above two scriptural references. Therefore, no one in heaven or earth can claim to be exempt from God's jurisdiction, authority or words. You cannot hide behind your race, ethnicity, religion, national origin, or geographical location. It is ludicrous for any person to claim that he or she is above, beyond or exempt from God's theological realm or spiritual domain. Such a claim or denial requires a radical and irrational break with history and the world of reality.

> Therefore my people are gone into captivity,
> because they have no knowledge. (Isaiah 5:13)

> Where there is no vision, the people perish.
> (Proverbs 29:18)

> Behold, I send you forth as sheep in the midst
> of wolves; be ye therefore wise as serpents,
> and harmless as doves. (Matthews 10:16)

> Woe unto you, lawyers! for ye have taken away
> the key of knowledge: ye entered not in yourselves,
> and them that were entering in ye hindered. (Luke
> 11:52)
> Study to show thyself approved unto God,
> A workman that needeth not be ashamed,
> rightly dividing the word of truth. (2 Timothy 2:15)

> All scripture is given by inspiration of God, and is
> Profitable for doctrine, for reproof, for correction,
> for instruction in righteousness. (2 Timothy 3:16)

There is a gross lack of knowledge in general among the American population. There is also a gross lack of motivation to get an adequate education to be informed and successful in life. This lack of general knowledge is compounded by the lack of biblical theological knowledge. Good and useful public policies depend directly upon an adequate fund of comprehensive knowledge. There is an urgent need to institute policies to increase knowledge and educational opportunities in a substantial way in America.

Theological Responsibility

The biblical mandates for the theological responsibility for public policy and public actions are overwhelming. From the Book of Genesis through the Book of Revelation, God is calling the public theologians to be witnesses, watchmen, stewards, disciples, educators, liberators, healers, writers, counselors, guardians, evangelists, revivalists, preachers, priests, prophets, caretakers, human service providers, visionaries, mentors, reformers, trainers, and leaders. God is calling the public theologians, the public disciples, the believers in Christ. God is calling with urgency for you to respond before it is too late! What is hindering you from your calling? What is preventing you from fulfilling your sacred responsibility? Have you conformed to the world to the extent that you cannot hear your calling? Have you been so transformed by the world that you have lost your will and courage to rise to the heavenly calling and the high calling of God in Jesus Christ?

The following authoritative scripture from the highest authority, God the Creator, is provided to highlight the duties, responsibilities and the commandments of God for the public theologians, disciples and God's people in regards to public policy and public actions:

In the first book of the Bible and the first Chapter God commands the first man and the first woman to do five things:

> And God blessed them, and God said unto them, be fruitful, and multiply, and replenish the earth, and subdue it: and have dominion over the fish of the sea, and over the fowl of the air, and over every living thing that moveth upon the earth. (Genesis 1:27-28)

The Way out of Darkness

This scripture is very clear and specific that God puts the man and the woman in charge of the inhabitants of the earth. This scripture is sufficiently explicit to make public policy.

The following prophecy of Ezekiel has a very significant and haunting message for theologians and other religious practitioners. In order to get the full meaning the complete chapter of Ezekial 33 should be read:

> So thou, O son of man, I have set thee a watchman unto the house of Israel; therefore, thou shalt hear the word at my mouth, and warn them from me. (Ezekial 33:7)

The watchman's job was to be a lookout for danger and to warn the people of the danger. The watchman's duty was also to warn the wicked to turn from their iniquity and warn the wicked of the destructive consequences of their wickedness. If the watchman fails to warn the wicked, the blood of the wicked will be on the watchman's hand. The wicked may not heed the message of the watchman. However, the watchman must warn the wicked to deliver himself from the blame and consequences of wickedness. There is a duty for the righteous to warn the wicked whether they take heed or not.

The prophet Isaiah has a similar prophecy and message as noted below:

> I have set watchmen upon thy walls, O Jerusalem,
> which shall never hold their peace day nor night:
> ye that make mention of the Lord, keep not silence.
> (Isaiah 62:6)

According to Isaiah the watchmen have a constant duty, day and night, to be on the lookout for danger. And when he sees the danger, he must not be silent. But he must warn the people. Also, the watchman must posture or situate himself or herself in such a way that it will afford the optimum advantage and opportunity to be a watchman. The watchman must be in a strategic position to observe what is going on.

Based on the messages of Ezekiel and Isaiah, the public theologians must make sure that the following public policies remain in active force:

1. Theology <u>is not</u> and <u>must not</u> be indifferent towards evil and wickedness.

2. A full-time watch must be employed to be on vigilant lookout for evil and danger.

3. Theology must employ ways and means to prevent evil and danger.

4. Theology must employ an effective system to warn the people of evil and danger.

5. Theology must employ an effective system to combat evil and danger.

6. Theology must have a proactive policy to promote peace and prosperity.

Many evils and dangers to humanity can be detected in their embryonic stages. Effective watching can bring about early detection before the danger has reached lethal and monstrous proportion. It is infinitely more difficult to deal with and eradicate evils and dangers that have grown to monstrous proportion.

It is unfortunate and even tragic for a society or people who have had no watchmen or unfaithful and incompetent watchmen. In such a situation, it is likely that evil and dangers have been given a head start. In such a case, conflicts, confusion, corruption and violence begin to multiply. Crises increase and the people are more at risk when they have not had faithful watchmen.

Isaiah describes the unfaithful watchmen in graphic terms:
> His watchmen are blind: they are all dumb dogs, they cannot bark; sleeping, lying down, loving to slumber. (Isaiah 56:10)

It is critical to have competent faithful watchmen, full time; for the safety of the people and the security of the society.

It is possible that the church, itself, in this 21st century could be guilty as the unfaithful watchman. The church or many churches, could be blind, at ease, slumbering and sleeping and silent in the presence of great dangers. It is so easy for the church to mistake its rhythmic singing, dancing, praising and celebrations for obedience to God. The theologians and the churches must be reminded in this regard by the words of the prophet Amos:

> I hate, I despise your feast days, and I will not smell in your solemn assemblies. Though ye offer me burnt offerings, I will not accept them: Neither will I regard the peace offerings of your fat beasts. Take thou away from me the noise of thy songs; for I will not hear the melody of thy viols. But let judgment run down as waters, and righteousness as a mighty stream. (Amos 5:21-24)

This rebuke was against people who practiced religious rituals and ceremonies, but God was not pleased. It would be an interesting study to observe and analyze how sometimes, sincere individuals and churches, deviate from the Will of God and become privatized and self serving. They often abandon the mission of God and lose their way and not recognize that they are lost. This is very evident in individuals and groups who have withdrawn and retreated from the community and the public world of reality. This phenomenon can be observed in sectarian groups, cults, gangs, arrogance, pride, and addictive behaviors. We must be mindful that certain individuals and groups are capable of creating their own fictional and delusional world of reality. Human beings are capable of creating their own idol gods and worship them.

The truth cannot be reduced to relativistic thinking. Isaiah warns those who attempt to do so in the following pronouncement:

> Woe unto them that call evil good, and good evil;
> That put darkness for light, and light for darkness;
> That put bitter for sweet, and sweet for bitter!
> (Isaiah 5:20)

In order to help understand and get some insight into why people deviate from the Will of God and into addictive and delusional thinking not based on reality, consider proverbs 16:25:

> There is a way which seemeth right unto a man, but the end thereof is the ways of death.

However, the most helpful scripture in understanding self deceit, disobedience, sectarianism, cultism and idolatry is found in the words of Paul to the Romans:

> For I bear them record that they have a zeal of God, but not according to knowledge. For they being ignorant of God's righteousness, and going about to establish their own righteousness, have not submitted themselves to the righteousness of God. (Romans 10:2-3)

Paul is highly qualified to make this statement because he himself exercised great zeal in persecuting the Christians until his conversion on the Damascus Road. Paul was sincere and thought he was doing the right thing by persecuting the Christians. His actions were based on his own blindness and his own ignorance and self righteousness.

The same kind of zeal, ignorance, blindness, self righteousness, stubbornness, disobedience, and persecutions are running rampant in our society today. People deviate from God's will and the standards set by God when they ignore the word of God and become wise in their own eyes. (Isaiah 5:21) (Deuteronomy 12:8). It is tragic when this kind of thinking begin to infiltrate the laws and the public policy of the society. It is critical that the most enlightened theological knowledge be available for the making of public policy. Unsound thinking, unsound doctrines, and unsound policies wreak havoc, confusion, injustice, and chaos in society. There is no excuse for perpetuating this ignorance, darkness, and disobedience; because the light of the world, the way, the truth, and the life has come in Jesus Christ.

The Bible itself is a book of public theology. It is about God's public disclosure to the world in history. The message is revealed publicity to the people of the earth. God sent his prophets to speak to nations and the world. He sent the prophet Jonah to warn the non- Jewish city, Nineveh, to repent and be saved. God's love is universal to all people. The Apostle Paul took the Gospel to gentiles in Asia and Europe. He took the Gospel to the Asians, Greeks, and Romans.

The Holy Bible, the message of God, is not a private document to be limited, restricted and circumscribed. It is an urgent message that transcends private and public. It cannot be restricted to any locality, race, or nationality. It is universal. The very fact that ideas are circulating and the issue of restricting the Bible and the Gospel of Christ from the public sector, is an indication of our gross ignorance, moral decay, and spiritual degeneracy.

The whole Bible, overwhelmingly, mandates theological responsibility for public policy, considering the Bible's historical precedents, universal influence and authoritative validated mandates, how could any responsible government or leader for the people allow this vital unique salvation knowledge to be excluded from its deliberations and public policies? How can the theologians be so passive when religion and especially the Christian religion and believers are being restricted and discouraged to acknowledge their beliefs in public?

As a footnote to the puzzling questions above, the state of Georgia passed a law that allows the teaching of the Bible in the high schools in Georgia in 2006. In June 2007, the Georgia State Department of Education completed a curriculum for the Bible course to be taught. Incredibly, most of the people in Georgia are not aware that the law has been passed. Most of the high schools in Georgia have not made any preparation to make this course available for their students for the 2007-2008, school year. The news media has not informed the public. The public officials have not taken any leadership initiative in the implementation of this Bible course. The clergy and the theologians are silent. The school officials are confused and reluctant. The masses are preoccupied with other interests. Our children and our society are dying for lack of knowledge.

It is difficult to find an explanation to the strange ironies above. Why are Christian voices so silent when the American culture is being infiltrated and invaded with antidemocratic and antichrist influences? Why are the Christians acquiescent and cooperative with the anti Christ forces that are forcing validated religion away from the public square?

In regard to public theology, several other strange ironies must be mentioned. The Christian Association of Public Theologians (CAPT) and the Christian Institute of Public Theology (CIPT) were founded and incorporated in Atlanta, Georgia 2002. The two organizations are direct legacies of ITC (Interdenominational Theological Center) and Morehouse College of Atlanta, Georgia. The founder and president of CAPT and CIPT is a graduate of Morehouse College and ITC. However, the president of ITC did not want ITC to be associated with the two public theology organizations. In fact, brochures indicating CAPT's and CIPT's affiliation with ITC had to be changed by the insistence of Dr. Michael Battle, because he did not want anything in writing that would reflect an affiliation with the two organizations. In addition to that, Dr. Battle closed the ITC certificate in Theology Program extension at the Shiloh Missionary Baptist Church where students were being trained in public theology. And he failed to honor the contract with the instructor who was teaching the ITC courses at Shiloh Missionary Baptist Church. This is not a criticism or a judgment on Dr. Battle. These are facts in search of answers to strange and inexplicable ironies.

An ITC instructor of many years explained to me that it was unwise to use the name Christian in the two public theology organizations. He stated that Christian is an exclusive term to other religions. He also stated that many potential donors to faith-based organizations would not make a contribution because of the use of Christian in the names of the organizations. It is again ironic that a professing Christian who has been a Christian pastor in a Christian church and a Christian professor in a Christian theological seminary; objects to the public use of the term Christian and views Christian as being exclusive. ITC has six plus schools under its umbrella of theological education. All of those schools are Christian schools. ITC is a Christian theological seminary. The clandestine hiding and denying the name of Jesus Christ in public is a part of the inexplicable complex dilemma of private professing Christians. The preceding scenarios clearly represent a hypocritical and gross abdication from theological responsibility for public policy as well as public witness.

When there is a demand by an individual, a group, circumstances, political or theological correctness, that you deny and renounce the name of Jesus Christ, you are being propositioned to give up your soul. No one has the right, the authority or power to request your soul. You must never give up your soul. If holding on to your soul requires an extreme and difficult decision, you must make that decision.

Jesus gives us scriptures for difficult and extreme decisions below:

> And if thy right eye offend thee, pluck it out, and cast it from thee: for it is profitable for thee that one of thy members should perish, and not that thy whole body should be cast into hell. And if thy right hand offend thee, cut it off, and cast it from thee: for it is profitable for thee that one of they members should perish, and not that thy whole body should be cast into hell.
> (Matthew 5:29-30)

This notion of denying and renouncing the name of Jesus Christ must be resisted at all cost. You must hold on to your soul.

The Greatest Public Theologian

Jesus Christ is the greatest theologian the world has ever known. He taught as one having authority (Matthew 7:29). He is the greatest theologian because He declared after His resurrection that all power is given unto Him in heaven and in earth (Matthew 28:18). He stated, "I and my Father are one." (St. John 10:30). When Jesus walked the earth, He demonstrated a public ministry. He did not have a church and He was not confined to any special place for His ministry. The world is His parish.

Jesus gave clear instructions to his disciples for public theology:

> What I tell you in darkness, that speak ye in light: and what ye hear in the ear, that preach ye upon the house tops (Matthew 10:27)

> Go ye therefore, and teach all nations, baptizing them in the name of the Father, and the Son, and of the Holy Ghost. (Matthew 28:19)

> Go ye into all the world, and preach the gospel to every creature. (Mark 16:15)

> But ye shall receive power, after that the Holy Ghost Is come upon you: and ye shall be witnesses unto

Me both in Jerusalem, and in all Judea, and in Samaria, And unto the uttermost part of the earth. (Acts 1:8)

The Bible is a Book of Public Theology. Its message is clear. Jesus Christ has illustrated, demonstrated and fulfilled its truths and prophecies. The Bible is a blue print for human survival and human triumph in God. The riches and resources of God are inexhaustible. The mission of Christ is clear.

How shall we escape, if we neglect so great salvation. (Hebrews 2:3)

Bibliography/References

The Holy Bible (King James Version)

Buttrick, George Arthur (ed.). <u>The Interpreters Bible</u>. New York: Abingdon Press, 1952.

Benne, Robert. <u>The Paradoxical Vision, A Public Theology for the Twenty-first Century</u>. Augsburg: Fortress Press, 1995.

Bright, John. <u>A History of Israel</u>. Philadelphia: Westminster Press, 1972.

Brueggemann, Walter. <u>Biblical Perspectives on Evangelism</u>. Nashville: Abingdon Press, 1993.

Carter, Stephen L. <u>The Culture of Disbelief</u>. New York: Random House, 1994.

Dudley, Carl S. <u>Community Ministry</u>. The Alban Institute, 1991.

Fosdick, Harry Emerson. <u>The Modern Use of the Bible</u>. New York: McMillan Co., 1961.

Ford, David F. <u>The Modern Theologians</u>. Cambridge: Blackwell Publishers, 1989.

Franklin, Robert M. <u>Liberating Visions</u>. Minneapolis: Fortress Press, 1990.

Franklin, Robert M. <u>Another Day's Journey</u>. Minneapolis: Fortress Press, 1997.

Goleman, Daniel. Emotional Intelligence. New York: Bantam Books, 1995.

Huber, Robert V. (ed.). The Bible Through the Ages. Pleasantville, New York: Readers Digest Association, 1996.

Kerr, Hugh T. (2nd edit). Readings in Christian Thought. Nashville: Abingdon Press, 1990.

Mays, Benjamin E. Born to Rebel. New York: Charles Scribner's Sons, 1971.

Mbiti, John S. African Religions and Philosophy. Portsmouth: Heineman Education Publishers, 1990.

Mead, Frank S. Handbook of Denominations in the United States. Nashville: Abingdon Press, 1985.

Nessan, Craig L. Beyond Maintenance to Mission. Minneapolis, 1999.

Quarles, Benjamin. The Negro in the Making of America. New York: MacMillan Publishing Company, 1987.
Seymour, Jack L. (ed.). Contemporary Approaches to Christian Education. Nashville: Abingdon Press, 1982.

Spilka, Bernard. The Psychology of Religion. Englewood Cliff: Prentice-Hall, 1985.

Strong, James. The New Strongs Exhaustive Concordance. Nashville: Nelson Publishers, 1995.

Theimann, Ronald F. <u>Constructing a Public Theology</u>. Lousiville: John Knox Press, 1991.

Tillman, William M., Jr. <u>Understanding Christian Ethics</u>. Nashville: Broadman, 1998.

Thiroux, Jacques. <u>Ethics-Theory and Practice</u>. Upper Saddle River, New Jersey: Prentiss Hall, 1998.

Torbet, Robert G. <u>A History of the Baptists</u>. Valley Forge: Judson Press, 1950.

Washington, Booker T. <u>Up From Slavery</u>. Doubleday, Page and Company, 1901.

Washington, Booker T. <u>My Larger Education</u>. Doubleday, Page and Company, 1911.

Webb, Willie James. <u>Psychotrauma – The Human Injustice Crisis</u>. Lima, Ohio: Fairway Press, 1990.

Webb, Willie James. <u>God's Spiritual Prescriptions</u>. Bloomington: AuthorHouse, 2001.

Printed in the United States
111039LV00004B/28-135/P